R.Holme, del:

W.Hawkins sc.

The Base of the Tower of Redcliff Church, with a view of the Muniment Room over the North Porch.

Published for Longman & Rees, Dec.13,1802.

T0371111

King del.

Storer sculp.

Interior of a Room in Redcliff Church, where Chatterton is said to have found some Ancient Manuscripts.

Published for Longman & Rees Dec.r 13, 1802.

CAMBRIDGE LIBRARY COLLECTION

Books of enduring scholarly value

Literary Studies

This series provides a high-quality selection of early printings of literary works, textual editions, anthologies and literary criticism which are of lasting scholarly interest. Ranging from Old English to Shakespeare to early twentieth-century work from around the world, these books offer a valuable resource for scholars in reception history, textual editing, and literary studies.

The Life of Thomas Chatterton

The poet and forger Thomas Chatterton (1752–70) is known today to have been the author of the Rowley poems, a series of compositions in medieval English. Chatterton claimed to have transcribed them from manuscripts written by a fifteenth-century monk, Thomas Rowley. After Chatterton's tragic early death, however, debate raged about the provenance of the poems. This biography, published in 1789, engages powerfully in that debate. Scholar and cleric George Gregory (1754–1808) makes every effort to defend Chatterton against the accusations of forgery, tackling each objection point by point, not least the question of why eighteenth-century syntax appears in the Rowley poems. Paired with Cottle and Southey's three-volume collection of Chatterton's work (also reissued in this series), this book attests to the growth of his influence and remains relevant to students and scholars of English literature.

Cambridge University Press has long been a pioneer in the reissuing of out-of-print titles from its own backlist, producing digital reprints of books that are still sought after by scholars and students but could not be reprinted economically using traditional technology. The Cambridge Library Collection extends this activity to a wider range of books which are still of importance to researchers and professionals, either for the source material they contain, or as landmarks in the history of their academic discipline.

Drawing from the world-renowned collections in the Cambridge University Library and other partner libraries, and guided by the advice of experts in each subject area, Cambridge University Press is using state-of-the-art scanning machines in its own Printing House to capture the content of each book selected for inclusion. The files are processed to give a consistently clear, crisp image, and the books finished to the high quality standard for which the Press is recognised around the world. The latest print-on-demand technology ensures that the books will remain available indefinitely, and that orders for single or multiple copies can quickly be supplied.

The Cambridge Library Collection brings back to life books of enduring scholarly value (including out-of-copyright works originally issued by other publishers) across a wide range of disciplines in the humanities and social sciences and in science and technology.

The Life of
Thomas Chatterton

*With Criticisms on his Genius and Writings,
and a Concise View of the Controversy
Concerning Rowley's Poems*

GEORGE GREGORY

CAMBRIDGE
UNIVERSITY PRESS

University Printing House, Cambridge, CB2 8BS, United Kingdom

Published in the United States of America by Cambridge University Press, New York

Cambridge University Press is part of the University of Cambridge.
It furthers the University's mission by disseminating knowledge in the pursuit of
education, learning and research at the highest international levels of excellence.

www.cambridge.org
Information on this title: www.cambridge.org/9781108063357

© in this compilation Cambridge University Press 2013

This edition first published 1789
This digitally printed version 2013

ISBN 978-1-108-06335-7 Paperback

This book reproduces the text of the original edition. The content and language reflect
the beliefs, practices and terminology of their time, and have not been updated.

Cambridge University Press wishes to make clear that the book, unless originally published
by Cambridge, is not being republished by, in association or collaboration with, or
with the endorsement or approval of, the original publisher or its successors in title.

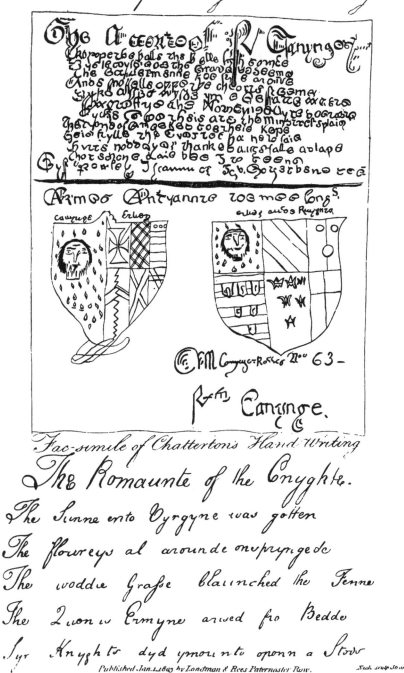

Fac simile of Rawley's Hand Writing.

Fac-simile of Chatterton's Hand Writing.

The Romaunte of the Cnyghte.

The Sunne ento Vyrgyne was gotten

The floureys al arounde onspryngede

The woddie Grasse blaunched the Fenne

The Lion is Ermyne arwed fro Bedde

Syr Knyghte dyd ymounte oponn a Stede

Published Jan. 1. 1803 by Longman & Rees Paternoster Row.

THE
LIFE
OF
THOMAS CHATTERTON,
WITH
CRITICISMS
ON HIS
GENIUS AND WRITINGS,
AND
A CONCISE VIEW
OF THE
CONTROVERSY
CONCERNING
ROWLEY's POEMS.

———

By G. GREGORY, D.D. F.A.S.
AUTHOR OF ESSAYS HISTORICAL AND MORAL, &c.

———

Agora com pobreza aborrecida,
    Por hofpicios alheos degradado;
Agora da efperança ja adquirida,
    De novo mais que nunca derribado.

CAMOENS.

———

LONDON.
PRINTED FOR G. KEARSLEY, No. 46, FLEET STREET.
1789.

[Price Five Shillings fewed.]

What are the Wages of the tuneful Nine,
What are their pleasures when compar'd to mine.
Happy I eat and toll my num'rous Pence,
Free from the Servitude of Rhime & Sense;
Tho' singsong Whitehead ushers in the year,
With Joy to Britain's King and Sovereign dear:
And in compliance to an anciont Mode,
Measures his Syllables into an Ode;
Yet such the scurvy Merit of his Muse,
He bows to Deans and licks his Lordship's Shoes
Then leave the wicked barren way of rhime,
Fly far from Poverty, be wise in time:
Regard the Office more, Parnassus less,
Put your religion in a decent dress:
Then may your Interest in the Town advance,
Above the reach of Muses or Romance.

ADVERTISEMENT.

THE following pages were compofed at the requeft of the refpectable Editor of the Biographia Britannica, in order to be inferted in that valuable work. The author, however, requefted leave to print off a fmall edition, in a feparate ftate, for the accommodaticn and fatisfaction of a few friends, to whom he was indebted on the occafion for fome valuable communications.

Perhaps the admirers of CHATTERTON, and thofe in particular who have interefted themfelves in the controverfy relating to Rowley's Poems, will not be difpleafed at feeing collected in one view all the particulars which are known concerning that extraordinary character.

The only claim to the public approbation, which the author prefumes to affert in favour of this little volume, is that of authenticity, as the public may reft affured that no fact has been admitted but upon the moft unexceptionable teftimony. He is not at liberty to publifh all his authorities, but whenever they are known he is confident in the affertion, that they will be found highly refpectable. The notes marked O. were added by a moft learned and intelligent friend, who honoured the manufcript with his perufal.

Entered at Stationers Hall.

[v]

TO THE RIGHT HON. THE

MARQUIS of LANSDOWN.

My LORD,

PERMIT me to introduce the unpatronifed
CHATTERTON to the only ftatefman of our
time who has manifefted a genuine zeal for
the promotion of literature and fcience. Had
the unfortunate fubject of thefe pages but
known, or had he made himfelf known to your
Lordfhip, there is much probability that the
world would at this day have continued to
enjoy the increafing fruits of his uncommon
talents.

It would, however, be the extreme of injuftice to confine your Lordfhip's commendation
to the exercife of private munificence, or the
admiration of learning. As one of that public, therefore, who are probably indebted for
every thing which they poffefs or enjoy, to the

wifdom

wifdom and virtue of your Lordfhip's adminiftration, allow me to unite with all the honeft and difcerning part of the community, in
expreffing my gratitude for the moft honourable and advantageous Peace which was ever
atchieved by this nation. When the little
contentions of Party are no more, and the
clouds of Faction are diffipated, the Friend of
Mankind and his Country will ftand confe-
crated to the veneration of pofterity; and it
will appear greater to have performed much
within a fhort period, than to have enjoyed
the emoluments of office for an age of inac-
tivity.

I have the honour to be,

    My Lord,

       With great refpect,

          Your Lordfhip's obliged

            And faithful Servant,

Winkworth Buildings,
May 20, 1789.   The Author.

THE

L I F E

O F

THOMAS CHATTERTON.

THE anceftry of men of genius is feldom of much importance to the public or
their biographers; the commonwealth of
literature is almoft a perfect democracy,
in which the rife or promotion of individuals is generally the confequence
of their refpective merits.   The family
of Chatterton, however, though in no
refpect illuftrious, is more nearly connected with fome of the circumftances
of his literary hiftory than that of moft
other votaries of the Mufes.—It appears
that the office of fexton of St. Mary

Redcliffe

Redcliffe, in Briftol, had continued in different branches of this family for more than one hundred and fifty years; and that John Chatterton, the laft of the name who enjoyed that office, was elected in March 1725, and continued fexton till his death, which happened in the year 1748 *. Thomas Chatterton, the nephew of the preceding, and father to the extraordinary perfon who is the fubject of thefe memoirs, had, we are informed, been in the early part of life in the ftation of a writing ufher to a claffical fchool †, was afterwards engaged as a finging man of the Cathedral of Briftol, and latterly was mafter of the free fchool in Pyle-ftreet in the fame city ‡. He died in Auguft 1752 ‖,

leaving

* Dr. Milles's Preliminary Differtation to Rowley's Poems, page 6.

† Ibid.

‡ Ib. Mr. Bryant's Obf. p. 514.

‖ Ibid.

leaving his wife then pregnant of a fon, who was born on the 20th of November, and baptized the 1ſt of January following, by the name of THOMAS, at St. Mary Redcliffe, by the Rev. Mr. Gibbs, vicar of that church.

The life of Chatterton, though ſhort, was eventful; it commenced as it ended, in indigence and misfortune. By the premature loſs of his father he was deprived of that careful attention which would probably have conducted his early years through all the difficulties that circumſtances or diſpoſition might oppoſe to the attainment of knowledge; and by the unpromiſing aſpect of his infant faculties he was excluded a feminary, which might have afforded advantages fuperior to thoſe he afterwards enjoyed. His father had been ſucceeded in the ſchool at Pyle-ſtreet by a Mr. Love, and to his care Chatterton was committed at the age

of

of five years ; but either his faculties were not yet opened, or the waywardnefs of genius, which will purfue only fuch ob-jects as are felf-approved, incapacitated him from receiving inftruction in the or-dinary methods ; and he was remanded to his mother as a dull boy, and incapable of improvement *. Nothing is more fal-lacious than the judgments which are formed during infancy of the future abili-ties of youth. Mrs. Chatterton was ren-dered extremely unhappy by the apparently tardy underftanding of her fon, till *he fell in love*, as fhe expreffed herfelf, with the illuminated capitals of an old mufical ma-nufcript, in French, which enabled her, by taking advantage of the momentary paffion, to initiate him in the alphabet †. She taught him afterwards to read from an old black-lettered Teftament, or Bible ‡.

Perhaps

---

* Bryant's Obfervations, p. 519.
† Ib. Milles's Prelim. Diff. p. 5.
‡ Milles's Prelim. Diff. p. 5.

Perhaps the bent of moſt men's ſtudies
may, in ſome meaſure, be determined by
accident, and frequently in very early life;
nor is it unreaſonable to ſuppoſe that his
peculiar attachment to antiquities may, in
a conſiderable degree, have reſulted from
this little circumſtance.

We are not informed by what means or
by what recommendation he gained ad-
miſſion into Colſton's charity-ſchool; but
doubtleſs, in the ſituation of his mother
at the time, it muſt have been a moſt de-
ſirable event; however unſuitable ſuch a
courſe of diſcipline might be to the improvement of Chatterton's peculiar talents.
Moſt of thoſe prodigies of genius, who
had hitherto aſtoniſhed mankind, by the
early diſplay of abilities and learning, had
been aided by the advantage of able in-
ſtructors, or had at leaſt been left at liberty
to purſue the impulſe of their ſuperior
underſtandings; it was the lot of Chatter-

ton

ton to be confined to the mechanical
drudgery of a charity-fchool; and the little
ordinary portions of leifure, with which
boys in his fituation are indulged, was the
only time allowed him to lay the foundation of that extenfive and abftrufe erudition
which decorated even his early years.
This feminary, founded by Edward Colfton, Efq. is fituate at St. Auguftine's
Back in Briftol, and is much upon the
fame plan with Chrift's Hofpital in London, (the only plan perhaps on which a
charity-fchool can be generally ufeful,)
the boys being *boarded* in the houfe,
clothed, and taught reading, writing, and
arithmetic. Chatterton, at this period,
wanted a few months of eight years of age,
being admitted on the 3d of Auguft 1760*.

The

* On the authority of a letter figned G. B. dated Briftol,
Auguft 30, 1778, printed in the St. James's Chronicle. In
Dr. Milles's Prelim. Diff. it is 1761; but this muft be a
mifprint, as all agree that he was between feven and eight
years old when admitted.

The rules of this inftitution are ftrict. The fchool hours in fummer are from feven o'clock till twelve in the morning, and from one till five in the afternoon; and in winter, from eight to twelve, and from one to four. The boys are obliged to be in bed every night in the year at eight o'clock, and are never permitted to be abfent from fchool, except on Saturdays and Saints days, and then only from between one and two in the afternoon till between feven and eight in the evening. The detail of thefe apparently trivial particulars may at prefent favour of a culpable minutenefs; but their importance will be experienced before I have concluded.

The firft years of his refidence at this feminary paffed without notice, and perhaps without effort. His fifter, indeed, in her letter to Mr. Croft, remarks, that he very early difcovered a thirft for preeminence, and that even before he was

B 4 five

five years old he was accuftomed to prefide
over his play-mates *.   There is a curious
letter from Mr. Thiftlethwaite of Briftol,
publifhed by Dr. Milles in his edition of
Rowley's Poems, which contains many
interefting particulars concerning Chatterton. In the fummer of 1763, Mr. Thiftlethwaite, who was then very young, contracted an intimacy with one Thomas
Philips †, an ufher or affiftant-mafter at
Colfton's fchool.   Though the education
of Philips had not been the moft liberal,
he

---

* Love and Madnefs, p. 161.   There is an anecdote of
Chatterton (it is given, however, only on a vague and in-
diftinct report) partly to the fame purpofe.   When very
young, a manufacturer promifed to make Mrs. Chatterton's
children a prefent of fome earthen-ware ; on afking the boy
what device he would have painted on his—" Paint me
(faid he) an angel, with wings, and a trumpet, to trumpet
my name over the world."

† In all probability the perfon on whofe death Chatterton
compofed an Elegy.   I wifh we were poffeffed of more perfect memoirs of Philips.   His tafte fo poetry excited a fimilar flame in feveral young men, who made no mean figure
in the periodical publications of that day, in Chatterton,
Thiftlethwaite, Cary, Fowler, and others.

he yet pofleffed a tafte for hiftory and poetry; and by his attempts in verfe, excited a degree of literary emulation among the elder boys. It is very remarkable, that Chatterton is faid to have appeared altogether as an idle fpectator of thefe poetical contefts; he fimply contented himfeif with the fports and paftimes which appeared more immediately adapted to his age; he apparently pofleffed neither inclination nor ability for literary purfuits, nor does Mr. Thiftlethwaite believe that he attempted a fingle couplet during the firft three years of his acquaintance with him* Whatever grounds Mr. Thiftlethwaite might have for this opinion, it, however, only ferves to furnifh an additional proof of the deceitfulnefs of thofe conjectures which are formed concerning the abilities of youth. The pert and forward boy, of active, but

fuperficial

---

* Milles's Rowley, p. 454.

fuperficial talents, generally bears away
the palm from the modefty and penfivenefs
of genius.   Such a difpofition, which is
in reality the refult of infenfibility, too
frequently meets with encouragement,
which produces indolence, impudence,
and diffipation ; while the lefs fhewy, but
more excellent underftandings, are depreffed by neglect, or difheartened by difcou-
ragement.   Chatterton, doubtlefs, at that
very period, was poffeffed of a vigour of
underftanding, of a quicknefs of penetration, a boldnefs of imagination, far fuperior to the talents of his companions.
But that penetration itfelf led him, perhaps, to feel more ftrongly his own de-
ficiences ; thofe delicate, yet vivid feelings which ufually accompany real abilities, induced him to decline a conteft, in
which there was a danger of experiencing
the mortification of being inferior.   If he
produced any compofitions, his exquifite

tafte

tafte led him to fupprefs them. In the
mean time he was laying in ftores of information, and improving both his imagination and his judgment. About his tenth
year he acquired a tafte for reading; and
out of the trifle, which was allowed him
by his mother for pocket-money, he began to hire books from a circulating library.
As his tafte was different from children
of his age, his difpofitions were alfo different. Inftead of the thoughtlefs levity
of childhood, he poffeffed the gravity,
penfivenefs, and melancholy of maturer
life. His fpirits were uneven; he was
frequently fo loft in contemplation, that
for many days together he would fay very
little, and apparently by conftraint. His
intimates in the fchool were few, and
thofe of the moft ferious caft. Between
his eleventh and twelfth year, he wrote a
Catalogue of the Books he had read, to
the number of feventy. It is rather unfortunate

fortunate that this Catalogue was not preferved; his fifter only informs us that they
principally confifted of hiftory and divinity *. At the hours allotted him for play,
he generally retired to read, and he was
particularly folicitous to borrow books †.
Though he does not appear to have manifefted any violent inclination to difplay his
abilities, yet we have undoubted proofs
that very early in life, he did not fail to
exercife himfelf in compofition. His
fifter having made him a prefent of a
pocket-book as a New-Year's gift, he returned it to her at the end of the year
filled with writing, chiefly poetry ‡. It
was probably from the remains of this
pocket-book, that the author of Love and
Madnefs tranfcribed a poem, which appears by the date (April 14th, 1764) to
have

---

* Mrs. Newton's Letter in Love and Madnefs.
† Dr. Milles's Prelim. Diff. page 5.
‡ Mrs. Newton's Letter.

have been written at the age of eleven
years and a half* This fact is certainly
a ftrong

* It may not be improper to produce this poem, not only as
it is the earlieft exifting fpecimen of Chatterton's compofitions, but alfo for the fake of fome remarks, which will probably throw fome light on the genius and character of its
author.

APOSTATE WILL, by T. C.

In days of old, when Wefley's pow'r
Gather'd new ftrength by every hour;
Apoftate Will juft funk in trade,
Refolv'd his bargain fhould be made;
Then ftrait to Wefley he repairs,
And puts on grave and folemn airs,
Then thus the pious man addrefs'd,
Good Sir, I think your doctrine beft,
Your fervant will a Wefley be,
Therefore the principles teach me.
The preacher then inftructions gave,
How he in this world fhould behave,
He hears, affents, and gives a nod,
Says every word's the word of God.
Then lifting his diffembling eyes,
How bleffed is the fect he cries,
Nor Bingham, Young, nor Stillingfleet
Shall make me from this fect retreat.
He then his circumftance declar'd,
How hardly with him matters far'd,
Begg'd him next meeting for to make
A fmall collection for his fake;

The

a ftrong contradiction to Mr. Thiftlethwaite's affertion, yet perhaps it is not

on

The preacher faid, do not repine,
The whole collection fhall be thine.
With looks demure and cringing bows,
About his bufinefs ftrait he goes ;
His outward acts were grave and prim,
The Methodift appear'd in him ;
But, be his outward what it will,
His heart was an Apoftate's ftill ;
He'd oft profefs an hallow'd flame,
And every where preach'd Wefley's name ;
He was a preacher and what not,
As long as money could be got ;
He'd oft profefs with holy fire,
The labourer's worthy of his hire.

It happen'd once upon a time,
When all his works were in their prime,
A noble place appear'd in view,
Then——to the Methodifts, adieu ;
A Methodift no more he'll be,
The Proteftants ferve beft for *he* ;
Then to the curate ftrait he ran,
And thus addrefs'd the rev'rend man ;
I was a Methodift, 'tis true,
With penitence I turn to you ;
O that it were your bounteous will
That I the vacant place might fill !
With juftice I'd myfelf acquit,
Do every thing that's right and fit.

The

on the whole fo difficult to be reconciled
as may at firft be fufpected.   In the regifters
of

> The curate ftraitway gave confent——
> To take the place he quickly went.
> Accordingly he took the place,
> And keeps it with diffembled grace.

April 14, 1764.

In the firft place, this poem fhews the early turn and
bent of his genius to fatire, which predominated throughout
his fhort life, and with which he began and ended his literary career.   Not only his fchool-fellows and his inftructors
became the fubjects of it at this early period, but his acquaintance and his friends felt its force.

In the next place, it appears that he was then no ftranger
to the works of Bingham, Young, and Stillingfleet, which
were probably among the books of divinity that compofed
the lift of thofe he had read or confulted, as mentioned in
Mrs. Newton's Letter.

Laftly, let it be obferved, that the perfon he fatirizes
is fuppofed to have turned methodift for mercenary mo-
tives, and to have preached the gofpel merely to put
money in his purfe.—Now Mr. Thiftlethwaite, in his letter
to Dean Milles, after mentioning Chatterton's intentions
of leaving his mafter's fervice and going to London,
fays—" I interrogated him as to the objects of his views
and expectations, and what mode of life he intended to purfue on his arrival at London.   The anfwer I received was a
memorable one : My firft attempt, faid he, fhall be in the
literary way ; the promifes I have received are fufficient to
difpel doubt ; but fhould I, contrary to my expectations,
find

of the memory, a few months is but a'
trifling anachronifm; befides, tho' Chatterton might compofe at that time, it
does not follow that he was under any neceffity of imparting his compofitions to
Mr. Thiftlethwaite or Mr. Philips; indeed, he was the lefs likely to make them
public, as they were of the fatirical kind,
and confequently, if difcovered, the boy
might

find myfelf deceived, I will in that cafe turn Methodift
preacher: Credulity is as potent a deity as ever, and a new
fect may eafily be devifed," &c.——*Milles's Rowley*,
page 459.

Chatterton might in fome meafure have in view the character which he had before fo fuccefsfully depicted, when he
thus expreffed himfelf to Mr. Thiftlethwaite. As his genius
was verfatile, and his reading extenfive, it is poffible this
profeffion might not be without fome ferious foundation;
indeed, if we are to believe that the fragment of a fermon,
which he produced as Rowley's, was really his own compofition, certainly many a quack preacher fets out upon a
much flenderer ftock of divinity than Chatterton was mafter
of at that time. The imagination, however, forms many
fchemes which the heart wants fortitude to reduce to action;
and perhaps, after all, his declaration to Mr. T. might be
no more than a temporary piece of gaiety, and that he
might ftill, though releafed from religious fcruples, abhor
the difhonourable character of a hypocrite.

might be apprehenfive of expofing himfelf
to punifhment.

At twelve years old he was confirmed
by the Bifhop: His fifter adds, that he
made very fenfible and ferious remarks on
the awfulnefs of the ceremony, and on
his own feelings preparatory to it *
Happy had it been for him if thefe fentiments, fo congenial to the amiable difpofitions of youth, had continued to influence his conduct during his maturer years.
He foon after, during the week in which
he was door-keeper, made fome verfes on
the laft day, paraphrafed the ninth chapter
of Job, and fome chapters of Ifaiah. The
bent of his genius, however, more ftrongly
inclined him to fatire, of which he was
tolerably lavifh on his fchool-fellows, nor
did the upper-mafter, Mr. Warner, efcape
the rod of his reprehenfion. The firft

C poetical

* Mrs. Newton's Letter.

poetical essays of most young authors are
in the pastoral style, when the imagination
is luxuriant, the hopes and contemplations
romantic, and when the mind is better
acquainted with the objects of nature and
of the sight than with any other; but
Chatterton, without the advantages of
education or encouragement, and, on these
accounts, diffident perhaps of his own
powers, wanted the stimulative of indignation to prompt him to action; and a
quickness of resentment appears through
life to have been one of his most distin-
guishing characteristics *. From what has
been related, it is probable that Chatterton was no great favourite with Mr. Warner; he, however, found a friend in the
under-

* A late French writer, in his Memoirs of the poet De
la Harpe, who had manifested a like turn for satire in his
early year , says—" La satyre est la premiere qualité qui se
develope ordinairement dans un jeune poete. Celui se
l'exerce d'unefaçon ridicule envers ses maitres & meme
envers M. Assalin."

under-mafter, Mr. Haynes, who conceived for him, I have been informed, a ftrong and affectionate attachment.

A very remarkable fact is recorded by Mr. Thiftlethwaite in the letter already quoted. " Going down Horfe-ftreet, near the fchool, one day," fays he, " I accidentally met with Chatterton. Entering into converfation with him, the fubject of which I do not now recollect, he informed me that he was in the poffeffion of certain old manufcripts, which had been found depofited in a cheft in Redcliffe church, and that he had lent fome or one of them to Philips. Within a day or two after this I faw Philips, and repeated to him the information I had received from Chatterton. Philips produced a manufcript on parchment or vellum, which I am confident was Elenoure and Juga *,

C 2   a kind

---

* See Rowley's Poems, p. 19, third edition.

a kind of paftoral eclogue, afterwards publifhed in the Town and Country Magazine
for May 1769.   The parchment or vellum appeared to have been clofely pared
round the margin; for what purpofe, or
by what accident, I know not, but the
words were evidently entire and unmuti-
lated.   As the writing was yellow and
pale, manifeftly (as I conceive) occafioned
by age, and confequently difficult to de-
cypher, Philips had with his pen traced
and gone over feveral of the lines, (which,
as far as my recollection ferves, were
written in the manner of profe, and without any regard to punctuation,) and by
that means laboured to attain the object of
his purfuit, an inveftigation of their meaning.   I endeavoured to affift him ; but
from an almoft total ignorance of the characters, manners, language, and orthography of the age in which the lines were
written, all our efforts were unprofitably
exerted ;

exerted, and though we arrived at the explanation of, and connected many of the words, ftill the fenfe was notorioufly deficient *." If this narrative may be depended on, Chatterton had difcovered thefe manufcripts before he was twelve years of age. It is, however, fcarcely confiftent with other accounts, fince both Mrs. Chatterton and her daughter feem to be of opinion, that he knew nothing of the parchments brought from Redcliffe church, which were fuppofed to contain Rowley's poems, till after he had left fchool †.

Under all the difadvantages of education, the acquifitions of Chatterton were furprifing. Befides the variety of reading which he had gone through, the author of Love and Madnefs remarks, he had fome

C 3   knowledge

---

* Milles's Rowley.

† Milles' Prelim. Diff. p. 5. There appears good reafon for fufpecting fome miftake in Mr. Thiftlethwaite's narrative, either as to the date, or fome other circumftance.

knowledge of mufic *.—Is it not probable that a few of the rudiments of vocal mufic made a part of the education of a charity boy? He had alfo acquired a tafte for drawing, which afterwards he greatly improved; and the ufher of the fchool afferted he had made a rapid progrefs in arithmetic † Soon atter ne left fchool, he correfponded with a boy, who had been his bed-fellow while at Colfton's, and was bound apprentice to a merchant at New-York ‡. Mrs. Newton fays, he read a letter at home, which he wrote to this friend; it confifted of a collection of all the hard words in the Englifh language, and he requefted his friend to anfwer it in

the

* Love and Madnefs, p. 167.

† Ibid. p. 161.

‡ At the defire of this friend, he wrote love verfes to be tranfmitted to him, and exhibited as his own. It is remarkable, that when firft queftioned concerning the old poems, he faid he was engaged to tranfcribe them for a gentleman, who alfo employed him to write verfes on a lady with whom he was in love.

the fame ftyle. An extraordinary effect of his difcovering an employment adapted to his genius is remarked in the fame letter. He had been gloomy from the time he began to learn, but it was obferved that he became more cheerful after he began to write poetry *.

On the 1ft of July 1767, he left the charity-fchool, and was bound apprentice to Mr. John Lambert, attorney, of Briftol, for feven years, to learn the art and myftery of a fcrivener. The apprentice fee was ten pounds; the mafter was to find him in meat, drink, lodging, and clothes; the mother in wafhing and mending. He flept in the fame room with the foot-boy, and went every morning at eight o'clock to the office, which was at fome diftance, and, except the ufual time for dinner, continued there till eight o clock at night,

C 4   after

---

† Milles's Prelim. Diff. p. 5.

after which he was at liberty till ten, when he was always expected to be at home. Mr. Lambert affords the most honourable testimony in Chatterton's favour, with respect to the regularity of his attendance, as he never exceeded the limited hours but once, when he had leave to spend the evening with his mother and some friends *. His hours of leisure also Mr. Lambert had no reason to suspect were spent in improper company, but generally with his mother, Mr. Clayfield, Mr. Barrett, or Mr. Catcott. He never had occasion to charge him with neglect of business, or any ill behaviour whatever. Once, and but once, he thought himself under the necessity of correcting him, and that was the pure effect of his disposition for satire. A short time after he was bound to Mr. Lambert, his old schoolmaster received a

very

* Mrs. Newton's Letter above quoted.

very abufive anonymous letter, which he
fufpected came from Chatterton, and he
complained of it to his mafter, who
was foon convinced of the juftice of the
complaint, not only from the hand-writing,
which was ill-difguifed *, but from the
letter being written on the fame paper
with that which was ufed in the office. On
this occafion Mr. Lambert corrected the
boy with a blow or two. He, however,
accufes him of a fullen and gloomy temper, which particularly difplayed itfelf
among the fervants †. Chatterton's fuperior abilities, and fuperior information,
with the pride which ufually accompanies
thefe qualities, doubtlefs rendered him an
unfit inhabitant of the kitchen, where his
ignorant

---

* This circumftance is not unworthy of notice. If Chatterton was really the forger of the MSS. attributed to
Rowley, how came he in this inftance to be unable to dif-
guife his own hand-writing?

† From the information of Mr. Lambert to a friend of
the author,

ignorant affociates would naturally be inclined to envy, and would affect to defpife
thofe accomplifhments, which he held in the
higheft eftimation ; and even the familiarity of vulgar and illiterate perfons, muft undoubtedly be rather difgufting than agreeable to a mind like his.

Mr. Lambert's was a fituation not unfavourable to the cultivation of his genius.
Though much confined, he had much
leifure. His mafter's bufinefs confumed a
very fmall portion of his time ; frequently, his fifter fays, it did not engage him
above two hours in a day *. While Mr.
Lambert was from home, and no particular bufinefs interfered, his ftated employment was to copy precedents ; a book of
which, containing 344 large folio pages,
clofely written by Chatterton while he remained in the office, is, I believe, ftill
in the poffeffion of Mr. Lambert, as
                                                 well

* Mrs. Newton's Letter above quoted.

well as another of about 30 pages.
The office library contained nothing
but law books; except an old edition
of Cambden's Britannia.   There is no
doubt, however, but Chatterton took
care amply to fupply his mental wants
from his old acquaintance at the circulating libraries.

He had continued this courfe of life for
upwards of a year; not, however, without fome fymptoms of an averfion for his
profeffion, before he began to attract the
notice of the literary world.   In the beginning of October 1768, the new bridge
at Briftol was finifhed; at that time there
appeared, in Farley's Briftol Journal, an
account of the ceremonies on opening the
old bridge, introduced by a letter to the
printer, intimating that " The following
defcription of *the Fryars firft paffing over
the old bridge,* was taken from an ancient
manufcript," and figned " Dunhelmus Brif-
tolien-

tolienfis *." The paper, if it be allowed to be the fabrication of modern times, demonftrates ftrong powers of invention, and an uncommon knowledge of ancient cuftoms.

* " Defcription of the Fryars paffing over the Old Bridge,
    " taken from an ancient manufcript.

" On Fridaie was the time fixed for paffing the new-
" brydge. Aboute the time of tollynge the tenth clocke,
" Mafter Greggoire Dalbenye mounted on a fergreyne
" horfe, informed Mafter Maier all thynges were pre-
" pared, when two Beadils went firft ftreying ftre. Next
" came a manne dreffed up as follows, hofe of gootfkyne
" crinepart outwards, doublette & waifcot, alfo over which
" a white robe without fleeves, much like an albe but not
" fo long, reachinge but to his hands. A girdle of azure
" over his left fhoulder, rechede alfo to his hands on the
" right & doubled back to his left, bucklynge with a goulden
" buckle dangled to his knee, thereby reprefentinge a Saxon
" earlderman.

" In his hands he bare a fhield, the maiftre of Gille a
" Brogton, who painted the fame, reprefenting Sainte
" Warburgh croffing the foorde ; then a mickle ftrong man
" in armour, carried a huge anlace, after whom came fix
" claryons & fix minftrels, who fong the fong of Sainte
" Warburgh. Then came Mafter Maier mounted on a
" white horfe dight with fable trappyngs wrought about by
" the Nunnes of Saint Kenna, with gould and Silver, his
" hayre braded with ribbons & a chaperon with the auntient
" armes of Briftowe faftened on his forehead. Mafter Mair
" bare in his hande a goulden rodde, & a congean fquire
                                        " bare

toms. So fingular a memoir could not fail to excite curiofity, and many perfons became anxious to fee the original. The printer, Mr. Farley, could give no account of

" bare in his hande, his helmet waulkinge by the fyde of
" the horfe. Then came the earlderman & city broders,
" mounted on fabyell horfes dyght with white trappyngs &
" plumes & fcarlet caps & chaperons having thereon fable
" plumes ; after them, the preefts & frears, parifh mendicant
" & fecular, fome fyngynge Sainte Warburghs fonge,
" others foundynge clarions thereto & others fome qitri-
" alles.

" In thilke manner reachynge the brydge the manne
" with the anlace ftode on the fyrft top of a mounde, yreed
" in the midft of the brydge, than went up the manne
" with the fheelde, after him the minftrels & clarions ;
" and then the preeftes & freeres all in white albes,
" making a moft goodly fhewe, the maier & earldermen
" ftandinge rounde, they fonge with the found of claryons,
" the fonge of Sainte Baldwyne, which being done, the
" manne on the top threw with great myght his anlace into
" the fea & the clarions founded an auncient charge &
" forloyne. Then theie fong again the fong of Sainte
" Warburge, & proceeded up Xts hill to the croffe,
" where a Latin fermon was preached by Ralph de Blun-
" derville, & with found of clarion theye againe want to the
" brydge and there dined, fpendynge the reft of the daye
" in fports and plaies, the freers of Sainte Auguftyne doing
" the play of the knights of Briftow meekynge a great fire
" at night on Kynflate hill."

of it, nor of the perfon who brought the copy; but after much inquiry, it was dif-covered that the manufcript was brought by a youth between fifteen and fixteen years of age, of the name of Thomas Chatterton *. " To the threats of thofe who treated him (agreeably to his appearance) as a child, he returned nothing but haughti-nefs, and a refufal to give any account †." By milder ufage he was fomewhat foften-ed, and appeared inclined to give all the information in his power. He at firft al-ledged, that he was employed to tranfcribe the contents of certain ancient manufcripts by a gentleman, who alfo had engaged him to furnifh complimentary verfes, in-fcribed to a lady with whom that gentle-man was in love. On being further preffed, he at laft informed the inquirers, that he had received the paper in queftion, together with many other manufcripts, from his father,

---

* Preface to Rowley's Poems.
† Croft's Love and Madnefs, p, 145.

father, who had found them in a large
cheſt in the upper room over the chapel,
on the north ſide of Redcliffe church *
But a ſtill more circumſtantial account of
the diſcovery of theſe manuſcripts, is preſerved in Mr. Bryant's Obſervations on
Rowley's Poems.   Over the north porch
of St. Mary Redcliffe church, which was
founded, or at leaſt rebuilt, by Mr. W.
Canynge, (an eminent merchant of Briſtol
in the 15th century, and in the reign of
Edward the Fourth,) there is a kind of
muniment room, in which were depoſited
ſix or ſeven cheſts, one of which in particular was called *Mr. Canynge's cofre* † ;
this cheſt, it is ſaid, was ſecured by ſix
keys,

---

* See Mr. Catcott's account in the preface to Rowley's
poems.

† When rents were received and kept in ſpecie, it was
uſual for corporate bodies to keep the writings and rents of
eſtates left for particular purpoſes, in cheſts appropriated to
each particular benefaction, and called by the benefactor's
name ; ſeveral old cheſts of this kind are ſtill exiſting in the
Univerſity of Cambridge.   O.

keys, two of which were entrufted to the minifter and procurator of the church, two to the mayor, and one to each of the church-wardens. In procefs of time, however, the fix keys appear to have been loft; and about the year 1727, a notion prevailed that fome title deeds, and other writings of value, were contained in Mr. Canynge's cofre. In confequence of this opinion, an order of veftry was made, that the cheft fhould be opened under the in-fpection of an attorney; and that thofe writings which appeared of confequence, fhould be removed to the fouth porch of the church. The locks were therefore forced, and not only the principal cheft, but the others, which were alfo fuppofed to contain writings, were all broken open. The deeds immediately relating to the church were removed, and the other ma-nufcripts were left expofed as of no value. Confiderable depredations had, from time

to

to time, been committed upon them, by different perfons ; but the moſt infatiate of theſe plunderers was the father of Chatterton. His uncle being ſexton of St. Mary Redcliffe gave him free acceſs to the church. He carried off, from time to time, parcels of the parchments, and one time alone, with the aſſiſtance of his boys, is known to have filled a large baſket with them. They were depoſited in a cupboard in the ſchool, and employed for different purpoſes, ſuch as the covering of copy books, &c. ; in particular, Mr. Gibbs, the miniſter of the pariſh, having preſented the boys with twenty bibles, Mr. Chatterton, in order to preſerve theſe books from being damaged, covered them with ſome of the parchments. At his death, the widow being under a neceſſity of removing, carried the remainder of them to her own habitation. Of the diſcovery of their value by the younger Chatterton,

D   the

the account of Mr. Smith, a very intimate
acquaintance, which he gave to Dr. Glynn
of Cambridge, is too interefting to be
omitted. " When young Chatterton was
firft articled to Mr. Lambert, he ufed
frequently to come home to his mother,
by way of a fhort vifit. There, one day,
his eye was caught by one of thefe parchments, which had been converted into a
thread-paper. He found not only the
writing to be very old, the characters very
different from common characters, but
that the fubject therein treated was different
from common fubjects. Being naturally
of an inquifitive and curious turn, he was
very much ftruck with their appearance,
and, as might be expected, began to queftion his mother what thofe thread-papers
were, how fhe got them, and whence
they came. Upon farther enquiry, he was
led to a full difcovery of all the parchments

ments which remained *;" the bulk of
them confifted of poetical and other compofitions, by Mr. Canynge, and a particular friend of his, Thomas Rowley, whom
Chatterton at firft called a monk, and afterwards a fecular prieft of the fifteenth
century. Such, at leaft, appears to be
the account which Chatterton thought
proper to give, and which he wifhed to be
believed. It is, indeed, confirmed by the
teftimony of his mother and fifter. Mrs.
Chatterton informed a friend of the Dean
of Exeter, that on her removal from
Pyle-ftreet, fhe emptied the cupboard of
its contents, partly into a large long deal
box, where her hufband ufed to keep his
clothes, and partly into a fquare oak box
of a fmaller fize; carrying both with their
contents to her lodgings, where, according to her account, they continued neglected

D 2   and

* Bryant's Obfervations, p. 511—529.

and undifturbed, till her fon firft difcovered their value; who having examined
their contents, told his mother, ' that he
had found a treafure, and was fo glad
nothing could be like it.' That he then
removed all thefe parchments out of the
large long deal box, in which his father
ufed to keep his clothes, into the fquare
oak box : That he was perpetually ran-
facking every corner of the houfe for more
parchments, and, from time to time, carried
away thofe he had already found by pockets
full : That one day happening to fee
Clarke's Hiftory of the Bible covered with
one of thofe parchments, he fwore a great
oath, and ftripping the book, put the
cover into his pocket, and carried it away;
at the fame time ftripping a common little
Bible, but finding no writing upon the
cover, replaced it again very leifurely *

" Upon

---

* Milles's Prelim. Diff p. 7. It does not appear that
any of the parchments exhibited to Mr. Barrett. or Mr.
Catcott,

" Upon being informed of the manner in which his father had procured the parchments, he went himfelf to the place, and picked up four more, which, if Mrs. Chatterton rightly remembers, Mr. Barrett has at this time in his poffeffion *."

" Mrs. Newton, his fifter, being afked, if fhe remembers his having mentioned Rowley's poems, after the difcovery of the parchments; fays, that he was perpetually talking on that fubject, and once in particular, (about two years before he left Briftol) when a relation, one Mr. Stephens of Salifbury, made them a vifit, he talked of nothing elfe †."

Nearly about the time when the paper in Farley's Journal, concerning the old bridge, became the fubject of converfation,

D 3   as

___

Catcott, were of a fize fufficient for a covering for an octavo book, much lefs for a quarto or folio.   O.

* Milles's Prelim. Diff. p. 7.

† Ibid.

as Mr. Catcott of Briftol, a gentleman of
an inquifitive turn, and fond of reading,
was walking with a friend in Redcliffe
church, he was informed by him of feveral ancient pieces of poetry, which had
been found there, and which were in the
poffeffion of a young perfon with whom he
was acquainted. This perfon proved to
be Chatterton, to whom Mr. Catcott defired to be introduced. He accordingly
had an interview; and foon after obtained
from him, very readily, without any reward, the Briftow Tragedy *, Rowley's
Epitaph upon Mr. Canynge's anceftor †,
with fome other fmaller pieces. In a few
days he brought fome more, among which
was *the Yellow Roll.* About this period,
Mr. Barrett, a refpectable furgeon in Briftol, and a man of letters, had projected a
hiftory of his native city, and was anxi-
                                        oufly

* See Rowley's Poems, p. 44.
† Ibid. p. 277.

oully collecting materials for that work. Such a discovery, therefore, as that of Chatterton could scarcely escape the vigilance of Mr. Barrett's friends. The pieces in Mr. Catcott's possession, of which some were copies and some originals, were immediately communicated to Mr. Barrett, whose friendship and patronage by these means our young literary adventurer was fortunate enough to secure. During the first conversations which Mr. Catcott had with him, he heard him mention the names of most of the poems since printed, as being in his possession. He afterwards grew more suspicious and reserved; and it was but rarely, and with difficulty, that any more originals could be obtained from him. He confessed to Mr. Catcott that he had destroyed several; and some which he owned to have been in his possession, were never afterwards seen. One of these was the tragedy of the Apostate,

D 4 of

or which a small part only has been preserved by Mr. Barrett.   The subject of it
was the apoftatizing of a perfon from the
Chriftian to the Jewifh faith *.   Mr. Barrett, however, obtained from him at different times feveral fragments, fome of
them of a confiderable length; they are all
written upon vellum, and he afferted them
to be a part of the original manufcripts,
which he had obtained in the manner which
has been already related.   A *fac fimile* of
one of thefe fragments is publifhed in
Mr. Tyrwhitt's and Dr. Milles's editions
of Rowley's Poems; and the fragments in
profe, which are confiderably larger, we
are taught to expect in Mr. Barrett's Hiftory of Briftol.   In the fame work we are
alfo promifed " *A Difcorfe on Briftowe,*
and the other hiftorical pieces in profe,
which Chatterton at different times de-
livered

---

* Bryant's Obfervations, p. 517.

livered out, as copied from Rowley's manufcripts *."

The friendſhip of Mr. Barrett and Mr. Catcott was of confiderable advantage to Chatterton.   They fupplied him occafionally with money, as a compenfation for fome of the fragments of Rowley, with which he gratified them †.   He ſpent many agreeable hours in their company; and their acquaintance introduced him into a more refpectable line than he could eafily have attained without it.   His fifter remarks, that after he was introduced to thefe gentlemen, his ambition daily and perceptibly encreafed; and he would frequently

---

* Preface to Rowley's Poems, p. 11.   It is now faid that Mr. B. does not mean to infert any of thefe pieces in his Hiftory.

† Some of his later compofitions, however, demonftrate, that he was not thoroughly fatisfied with his Briftol patrons; and Mr. Thiftlethwaite does not hefitate to affert, that he felt himfelf greatly difappointed in his expectations of pecuniary rewards for his communications.   K.

quently fpeak in raptures of the undoubted
fuccefs of his plan for future life. " When
in fpirits, he would enjoy his rifing fame,
and, confident of advancement, he would
promife his mother and I fhould be par-
takers of his fuccefs *." Both thefe
gentlemen alfo lent him books ; Mr. Barrett lent him feveral medical authors †,
and, at his requeft, gave him fome in-
inftructions in furgery. His tafte was
verfatile, and his ftudies various. In the
courfe of the years 1768 and 1769, Mr.
Thiftlethwaite frequently faw him, and
defcribes in a lively manner the employment of his leifure hours. " One day,"
fays Mr. T. " he might be found bufily
employed in the ftudy of heraldry and
Englifh antiquities, both of which are
numbered among the moft favourite of his
                                    purfuits ;

* Mrs. Newton's letter before quoted.
† Ibid.

purfuits; the next difcovered him deeply
engaged, confounded and perplexed amidft
the fubtleties of metaphyfical difquifition,
or loft and bewildered in the abftrufe
labyrinth of mathematical refearches; and
thefe in an inftant again neglected and
thrown afide, to make room for mufic
and aftronomy, of both which fciences his
knowledge was entirely confined to theory.
Even phyfic was not without a charm to
allure his imagination, and he would talk
of Galen, Hippocrates, and Paracelfus,
with all the confidence and familiarity of a
modern empirick *." It may naturally be
fuppofed, that his acquaintance with moft
of thefe fciences was very fuperficial; but
his knowledge of antiquities was extenfive,
and we might perhaps fay profound. With
a view of perfectin himfelf in thefe favourite ftudies, he borrowed Skinner's
Etymologicon

* Milles's Rowley. p 456.

Etymologicon of Mr. Barrett, but returned it in a few days as ufelefs, moft of the
interpretations being in Latin.   He alfo
borrowed Benfon's Saxon Vocabulary, but
returned it immediately on the fame account *.   His difappointment was partly
compenfated by the acquifition of Ker-
fey's Dictionary, and Speght's Chaucer,
(the Gloffary to which he carefully
tranfcribed †.)   With thefe books he
was furnifhed by Mr. Green, a bookfeller in Briftol.   Probably the mortification he received at not being able to
make that ufe which he defired of Skinner
and of Benfon, might be an additional fti-
mulative to the great inclination which
he manifefted to acquaint himfelf with
Latin, and his defign to attempt it without a mafter.   From this project his friend,
Mr. Smith, took great pains to diffuade
him,

---

* Bryant's Obferv. p. 532.

† Milles's Prelim. Diff. p. 5, and 17.

him, and advifed him rather to apply to
French, a competent knowledge of which
might be fooner attained, and which promifed to be of more effential fervice *.
Whatever plan he adopted, he entered upon
it with an earneftnefs and fervour almoft un-
exampled. Indeed, the poetic enthufiafm was
never more ftrongly exhibited than in Chatterton.   Like Milton, he fancied he was
more capable of writing well at fome particular times than at others, and the full of
the moon was the feafon when he imagined
his genius to be in perfection; at which
period, as if the immediate prefence of that
luminary added to the infpiration, he frequently devoted a confiderable portion of
the night to compofition†.—" He was always," fays Mr. Smith, " extremely fond of
walking in the fields, particularly in Redcliffe meadows, and of talking about thefe
                                    (Row-

* Bryant's Obferv. p. 532.
† Mrs. Newton's letter to Mr. C.

(Rowley's) manufcripts, and fometimes reading them there. " Come (he would " fay) you and I will take a walk in the " meadow. I have got the clevereft thing " for you imaginable. It is worth half- " a crown merely to have a fight of it, " and to hear me read it to you." When we arrived at the place propofed, he would produce his parchment, fhew it and read it to me. There was one fpot in particu- lar, full in view of the church, in which he feemed to take a peculiar delight. He would frequently lay himfelf down, fix his eyes upon the church, and feem as if he were in a kind of trance. Then, on a fudden and abruptly, he would tell me, " that fteeple was burnt down by light- " ning : that was the place where they " formerly acted plays * " His Sundays were commonly fpent in walking alone in- to the country about Briftol, as far as the
duration

* Bryant's Obferv. p. 530.

duration of day-light would allow; and from thefe excurfions he never failed to bring home with him drawings of churches, or of fome other objects, which had impreffed his romantic imagination *.

His attention, while at Briftol, was not confined to Rowley; his pen was exercifed in a variety of pieces, chiefly fatirical, and feveral effays, both in profe and verfe, which he fent to the Magazines. I have not been able to trace any thing of Chatterton's in the Town and Country Magazine (with which he appears to have firft correfponded) before February 1769; but in the acknowledgments to correfpondents for November 1768, we find "D. B. of Briftol's favour will be gladly received."

Dunhelmus

---

* Love and Madnefs, p. 159. The Dean of Exeter mentions drawings by Rowley of Briftol Caftle, which he fuppofes genuine, but which Mr. Warton reprobates as fictions of Chatterton, the reprefentations of a building which never exifted, in a capricious, affected ftyle of Gothic architecture, reducible to no fyftem. O.

Dunhelmus Briftolienfis was the fignature
he generally employed. In the courfe of
the year 1769, he was a confiderable con-
tributor to that publication. One of the
firft of his pieces which appeared was a
letter on the tinctures of the Saxon heralds,
dated Briftol, February 4; and in the
fame Magazine a poem was inferted on
Mr. Alcock, of Briftol, an excellent miniature painter, figned *Afaphides* *. In the
fame Magazine for March are fome extracts from Rowley's manufcripts; and in
different numbers for the fucceeding
months, fome pieces called Saxon poems,
written in the ftyle of Offian.

The whole of Chatterton's life prefents
a fund of ufeful inftruction to young perfons of brilliant and lively talents, and
affords a ftrong diffuafive againft that impetuofity

* This piece, with two or three others in Chatterton's
Mifcellanies, was claimed by John Lockftone, a linen-
draper in Briftol, a great friend of Chatterton; by his confeffion, however, it was corrected by the latter.

petuofity of expectation, and thofe delufive hopes of fuccefs, founded upon the
confcioufnefs of genius and merit, which
lead them to neglect the ordinary means of
acquiring competence and independence.
The early difguft which Chatterton conceived for his profeffion, may be accounted one of the prime fources of his misfortunes. Among the efforts which he made
to extricate himfelf from this irkfome fituation, the moft remarkable is his application
to the Hon. Horace Walpole, in March
1769 * ; the ground of which was an offer
to furnifh him with fome accounts of a
feries of great painters, who had flourifhed
at Briftol, which Chatterton faid had been
lately difcovered, with fome old poems,
in that city. The pacquet fent by Chatterton was left at Bathurft's, Mr. Walpole's bookfeller, and contained, befide

E   this

* Two Letters by the Honourable Horace Walpole,
P. 55.

this letter, an ode or little poem, of two
or three ftanzas in alternate rhyme, on the
death of Richard I. as a fpecimen of the
poems which were found. Mr. Walpole had
but juft before been made the inftrument
of introducing into the world Mr. M'Pher-
fon's forgeries; a fimilar application, therefore, ferved at once to awaken his fufpicion. He, however, anfwered Chatterton's letter, defiring further information;
and in reply, was informed, that " he
(Chatterton) was the fon of a poor widow,
who fupported him with great difficulty;
that he was apprentice to an attorney, but
had a tafte for more elegant ftudies." The
letter hinted a wifh that Mr. Walpole
would affift him in emerging from fo dull
a profeffion, by procuring fome place, in
which he might purfue the natural bias
of his genius. He affirmed that great
treafures of ancient poetry had been difcovered at Briftol, and were in the hands
of a perfon who had lent him the fpecimen

men already tranſmitted, as well as a paſtoral (Elinoure and Juga) which accompanied this ſecond letter. Mr. Walpole
wrote to a friend, a noble lady at Bath,
to enquire after the author of theſe letters,
who found his account of himſelf verified
in every particular. In the mean time the
ſpecimens were communicated to Mr.
Gray and Mr. Maſon, and thoſe gentlemen, at firſt ſight, pronounced them
forgeries. Mr. Walpole, though convinced of the author's intention to impoſe
upon him, could not, as he himſelf con-
feſſes, help admiring the ſpirit of poetry
which animated theſe compoſitions. The
teſtimonies of his approbation, however,
were too cold to produce in Chatterton
any thing but laſting diſguſt. Mr. Walpole's reply was indeed (according to his
own account) rather too much in the
common-place ſtyle of Court replies;
though ſome allowance is to be made for

his peculiar fituation, and for his juſt apprehenfion of a new impofition to be prac-
tifed on him.   He complained in general
terms of his want of power to be a patron,
and advifed the young man to apply himfelf to the duties of his profeſſion, as more
certain means of attaining the independence
and leifure of which he was defirous.
This frigid reception extracted immediately from Chatterton, " a peevifh letter,"
defiring the manufcripts back, as they
were the property of another; and Mr.·
Walpole, either offended at the warm and
independent fpirit which was manifefted
by the boy, or pleafed to be difengaged
from the bufinefs in fo eafy a manner,
proceeded on a journey to Paris, without
taking any·further notice of him.   On
his return, which was not for fome time,
he found another epiftle from Chatterton,
in a ftyle (as he terms it) " fingularly impertinent ;" expreffive of much refentment

ment on account of the detention of his poems, roughly demanding them back, and adding, " that Mr. Walpole would not have *dared* to ufe him fo ill, had he not been acquainted with the narrownefs of his circumftances." The confequence was, therefore, fuch as might be expected. Mr. Walpole returned his poems and his letters in a blank cover, and never afterwards heard from him or of him during his life *. The affront was never forgiven by the difappointed poet, though it is perhaps more than repaid by the ridiculous portrait which he has exhibited of Mr. W———, in the Memoirs of a Sad Dog, under the character of " the redoubted Baron Otranto †, who has fpent his whole life in conjectures."

On the fcore of thefe tranfactions, Mr. Walpole has incurred more cenfure than

E 3 he

* Ib. paffim.
† Chat. Mifcel. p. 184.

he really deferved.   In an age when literature is fo little patronized by thofe who
wield all the powers of the ftate, and have
in truft for the public the diftribution of
its emoluments; when men of the firft,
abilities, actually engaged in the learned
profeffions, are permitted to languifh in
obfcurity and poverty, without any of thofe
rewards, which are *appropriated* to the
profeffions they exercife, and are compelled
to depend for a precarious fubfiftence on
the fcanty pittance, which they derive
from diurnal drudgery in the fervice of
bookfellers, it can fcarcely be deemed an
inftance of extraordinary illiberality that a
private man, though a man of fortune,
fhould be inattentive to the petition of a
perfect ftranger, a young man, whofe
birth or education entitled him to no high
pretenfions, and who had only conceived
an unreafonable diflike to a profeffion both
lucrative and refpectable.   If Chatterton

2   had

had actually avowed the poems, perhaps a
very generous and feeling heart, such as
rarely exifts at prefent, and leaft of all in
the higher circles of life, might have been
more ftrongly affected with their beauties,
and might probably have extended fome
fmall degree of encouragement. But con-
fidering things as they are, and not as they
ought to be, it was a degree of unufual
condefcenfion to take any notice whatever
of the application ; and when Chatterton
felt fo poignantly his difappointment, he
only demonftrated his ignorance of the
ftate of patronage in this country, and acted
like a young and ingenuous perfon, who
judged of the feelings of courtiers by the
generous emotions of his own breaft, or
the practice of times, which exift now only in the records of romance. Mr. Walpole afterwards regretted, and I believe fin-
cerely, that he had not feen this extraordinary youth, and that he did not pay a

more

more favourable attention to his correfpondence; but, to be neglected in life,
and regretted and admired when thefe
paffions can be no longer of fervice, has
been the ufual fate of learning and genius.
Mr. Walpole was certainly under no obligation of patronizing Chatterton.   To
have encouraged and befriended him, would
have been an exertion of liberality and munificence uncommon in the prefent day;
but to afcribe to Mr. Walpole's neglect
(if it can even merit fo harfh an appella-
tion) the dreadful cataftrophe, which happened at the diftance of nearly two years
after, would be the higheft degree of injuftice and abfurdity *.

The

* A learned and refpectable friend, on reading thefe memoirs in manufcript, favoured me with the following able
vindication of Mr. W. which, for the fatisfaction of thofe
who wifh for the fulleft information on the fubject, I infert
intire.

It has already been ftated, that, in March 1769, Chatterton, not long after his acquaintance with Mr. Barrett
and

The reader has hitherto contemplated Chatterton in the pleafing light of an ingenious

and Mr. Catcott, to whom he had communicated fome originals and fome tranfcripts of Rowley's Poems, wrote a letter to Mr. H. Walpole, inclofing alfo a fpecimen of the poems, and foliciting his patronage. Let the reader take the account in Mr. Walpole's own words, from an extract of a letter to Mr. W. B. added to another letter to the Editor of Chatterton's Mifcellanies, and printed at Strawberry-hill, 1779.

" I am far from determined to publifh any thing about
" Chatterton. It would almoft look like making myfelf a
" party. I do not love controverfy ; if I print, my chief
" reafon would be, that both in the account of the poems,
" and in Mr. Warton's laft volume, my name has been
" brought in with fo little circumfpection and accuracy,
" that it looks as if my rejection of Chatterton had driven
" him to defpair ; whereas I was the firft perfon on whom
" he effayed his art and ambition, inftead of being the
" laft. I never faw him ; there was an interval of near two
" years between his application to me and his difmal end ;
" nor had he quitted his mafter, nor was neceffitous, nor
" otherwife poor than attornies clerks ufually are ; nor had
" he come to London, nor launched into diffipation, when
" his correfpondence with me ftopped. As faithfully as I
" can recollect the circumftances, without dates, and
" without fearching for what few memorandums I pre-
" ferved relative to him, I will recapitulate his hiftory
" with me. Bathurft, my bookfeller, brought me a
" pacquet left with him ; it contained an ode, or little
" poem,

nious and virtuous youth. I reluctantly
proceed to develope the only circumſtance
which

" poem, of two or three ſtanzas in alternate rhyme, on the
" death of Richard the Firſt, and I was told, in very few
" lines, that it had been found at Briſtol, with many other
" old poems, and that the poſſeſſor could furniſh me with
" accounts of a ſeries of great painters, who had flouriſhed
" at Briſtol.

  " Here I muſt pauſe, to mention my own reflections.
" At firſt I concluded that ſomebody having met with my
" Anecdotes of Painting, had a mind to laugh at me ; I
" thought not very ingenuouſly, as I was not likely to
" ſwallow a ſucceſſion of great painters at Briſtol. The
" ode, or ſonnet *, as I think it was called, was too pretty
" to be part of the plan ; and, as is eaſy with all the other
" ſuppoſed poems of Rowley, it was not difficult to make it
" modern by changing the old words for new, though yet
" more difficult than with moſt of them. You ſee I tell you
" fairly the caſe.

  " I wrote, according to the incloſed direction, for farther
" particulars. Chatterton, in anſwer, informed me that
" he was the ſon of a poor widow, who ſupported him with
" great difficulty ; that he was clerk or apprentice to an at-
" torney, but had a taſte and turn for more elegant ſtudies ;
" and hinted a wiſh that I would aſſiſt him with my intereſt
" in emerging out of ſo dull a profeſſion, by procuring
" him ſome place, in which he could purſue his natural
" bent. He affirmed that great treaſures of ancient poetry
                                                      " had

* " Richard of Lyon's Heart to fight is gone."

which has involved his name and character in difgrace, and which certainly deprived

" had been difcovered in his native city, and were in the
" hands of a *perfon*, who had lent him thofe he had tranf-
" mitted to me ; for he now fent me others, amongft which
" was an abfolute modern paftoral in dialogue, thinly
" fprinkled with old words *.   Pray obferve, Sir, that he
" affirmed having received the poems from another perfon ;
" whereas it is afcertained that the gentleman at Briftol,
" who poffeffes the fund of Rowley's poems, received them
" from Chatterton.

    " I wrote to a relation of mine at Bath, to enquire into
" the fituation and charafter of Chatterton, according to
" his own account of himfelf ; nothing was returned about
" his charafter, but his ftory was verified.

    " In the mean time I communicated the poems to Mr.
" Gray and Mr. Mafon, who at once pronounced them
" forgeries, and declared there was no fymptom in them of
" their being the productions of near fo diftant an age ; the
" language and metres being totally unlike any thing an-
" cient.

    " Well, Sir, being fatisfied with my intelligence about
" Chatterton, I wrote him a letter with as much kindnefs
" and tendernefs as if I had been his guardian ; for though
" I had no doubt of his impofitions, fuch a fpirit of poetry
" breathed in his coinage, as interefted me for him ; nor
" was it a grave crime in a young bard to have forged falfe
" notes of hand, that were to pafs current only in the parifh
                                                    " of

* Elinoure and Juga.

prived the world prematurely of his excellent abilities.   When or how he was unfortunate

" of Parnaſſus.   I undecived him about my being a perſon
" of any intereſt, and urged, that in duty and gratitude to
" his mother, who had ſtraitened herſelf to breed him up to
" a profeſſion, he ought to labour in it, that in her old age
" he might abſolve his filial debt ; and I told him, that
" when he ſhould have made a fortune, he might unbend
" himſelf with the ſtudies conſonant to his inclinations.   I
" told him alſo, that I had communicated his tranſcripts to
" better judges, and that they were by no means ſatisfied
" with the authenticity of his ſuppoſed MSS.   He wrote
" me rather a peeviſh anſwer, ſaid he could not conteſt with
" a perſon of my learning, (a compliment by no means due
" to me, and which I certainly had not aſſumed, having
" mentioned my having conſulted abler judges,) main-
" tained the genuineneſs of the poems, and demanded to
" have them returned, *as they were the property of another*
" *gentleman*.   Remember this.
"   When I received this letter, I was going to Paris in a
" day or two, and either forgot his requeſt of the poems,
" or perhaps not having time to have them copied,
" deferred complying till my return, which was to be in
" ſix weeks.   I proteſt I do not remember which was the
" caſe ; and yet, though in a cauſe of ſo little importance,
" I will not utter a ſyllable of which I am not poſitively
" certain, nor will not charge my memory with a tittle be-
" yond what it retains.   Soon after my return from France,
" I received another letter from Chatterton, the ſtyle of
" which was ſingularly impertinent.   He demanded his
                                              " poems

fortunate enough to receive a tincture of
infidelity, we are not informed.   Early in
the

" poems roughly ; and added, that I fhould not have dared
" to ufe him fo ill, if he had not acquainted me with the
" narrownefs of his circumftances My heart did not accufe
" me of infolence to him.   I wrote an anfwer to him, ex-
" poftulating with him on his injuftice, and renewing good
" advice ; but upon fecond thoughts, reflecting that fo
" wrong-headed a young man, of whom I knew nothing,
" and whom I had never feen, might be abfurd enough to
" print my letter, I flung it into the fire ; and wrapping up
" both his poems and letters, without taking a copy of
" either, for which I am now forry, I returned all to him,
" and thought no more about him or them, till about a year
" and a half after, when dining at the Royal Academy,
" Dr. Goldfmith drew the attention of the company with
" an account of a marvellous treafure of ancient poems
" lately difcovered at Briftol, and expreffed enthufiaftic be-
" lief in them, for which he was laughed at by Dr. John-
" fon, who was prefent.   I foon found this was the trou-
" vaille of my friend Chatterton ; and I told Dr Goldfmith
" that this novelty was none to me, who might, if I had
" pleafed, have had the honour of uſhering the great dif-
" covery to the learned world.   You may imagine, Sir,
" we did not at all agree in the meafure of our faith ; but
" though his credulity diverted me, my mirth was foon
" daſhed ; for on aſking about Chatterton, he told me he
" had been in London, and had deftroyed himfelf.   I
" heartily wiſhed then that I had been the dupe of all the
" poor young man had written to me ; for who would not
                                        " have

the year 1769, it appears from a poem on
Happinefs, addreffed to Mr. Catcott, that
he

" have his underftanding impofed upon to fave a fellow
" being from the utmoft wretchednefs, defpair, and fuicide !
" and a poor young man, not eighteen, and of fuch miracu-
" lous talents ; for, dear Sir, if I wanted credulity on
" one hand, it is ample on the other.   Yet heap all the
" improbabilities you pleafe on the head of Chatterton, the
" impoffibility on Rowley's fide will remain.   An amazing
" genius for poetry, which one of them poffeffed, might
" flafh out in the darkeft age ; but could Rowley anticipate
" the phrafeology of the eighteenth century ?   His poetic
" fire might burft through the obftacles of the times ; like
" Homer, or other original bards, he might have formed
" a poetical ftyle ; but would it have been precifely that
" of an age fubfequent to him by fome hundred years ?
" Nobody can admire the poetry of the poems in queftion
" more than I do, but except being better than moft mo-
" dern verfes, in what do they differ in the conftruction ?
" The words are old, the conftruction evidently of yefter-
" day ; and, by fubftituting modern words, aye, fingle
" words, to the old, or to thofe invented by Chatterton,
" in what do they differ ?   Try that method with any com-
" pofition, even in profe, of the reign of Henry VI. and
" fee if the confequence will be the fame.   But I am get-
" ting into the controverfy, inftead of concluding my nar-
" rative, which indeed is ended."

   Whatever imputation might have lain on Mr. Walpole
with regard to the treatment of Chatterton, before thefe
particulars were known, and this narrative appeared, furely
there

he had drank deeply of the poifoned
fpring: And in the conclufion of a letter

to

there can be no impartial reader of it who will not acquit
him of any ill treatment of a perfon who appeared to him in
fo queftionable a fhape; and allow that in Mr. Walpole's
fituation, he could fcarcely have acted otherwife than he did.
For what was the cafe? A youth of fixteen years of age,
clerk to an attorney at Briftol, totally unknown to Mr.
Walpole, fends him a letter, acquainting him that the
writer, though bred to the law, had a tafte for politer ftudies,
particularly poetry, and wifhed to be drawn out of his
prefent fituation, and placed in one more at his eafe,
where he might purfue the ftudies more congenial to his tafte
and genius; but of this tafte and genius he produces no other
proof than tranfcripts of fome old poems, faid to have been
found at Briftol, and to be *the property of another perfon.*
Thefe poems being exhibited by Mr. Walpole to Mr. Gray
and Mr. Mafon, thefe excellent and impartial judges agreed
in opinion that they muft be modern productions, difguifed
in antiquated phrafes; and, with regard to a long lift of
Briftol artifts, carvellers and painters, announced alfo as
part of this treafure, Mr. Walpole was as confident that
none fuch ever had any exiftence, and therefore he could
not help concluding that the whole was a fiction, contrived
by fome one or more literary wags, who wifhed to impofe
on his credulity, and to laugh at him if they fucceeded, and
that Chatterton was only the inftrument employed to introduce and recommend thefe old writings. His youth and
fituation could not lead Mr. Walpole to fuppofe he was
himfelf the author and contriver, more efpecially as he had

afferted

to the fame gentleman, after he left Briftol, he expreffes himfelf: " Heaven fend
you

afferted them to be the property of a perfon at Briftol then
alive. He had indeed reprefented himfelf as a lover of
the mufes, but had given no fpecimens of his *own* compofitions: The kindeft thing therefore Mr. Walpole could do
for a young man in this fituation, was, after a gentle hint
of his fufpicions of the authenticity of the poems, to recommend to his correfpondent to purfue the line of bufinefs
in which he was placed, as moft likely to fecure a decent
maintenance for himfelf, and enable him to affift his mother. However difappointed Chatterton might have been
at the time, and angry with Mr. Walpole for this rebuff,
it fhould feem as if he had not harboured any long or ftrong
refentment againft that gentleman ; for in a copy of verfes
addreffed to Mifs M. R. and fent by him to the Town and
Country Magazine, and printed in the Number for January
1770, is the following ftanza :

" Yet when that bloom and dancing fire,
" In filver'd reverence fhall expire,
   " Aged, wrinkled, and defac'd,
" To keep one lover's flame alive
" Requires the genius of a *Clive*,
   " With WALPOLE's mental tafte.

See Chatterton's Mifcellanies, p. 88.

It fhould feem alfo, that Chatterton had in part adòpted
Mr. Walpole's advice, by continuing with his mafter a full
twelvemonth after his application to that gentlemen. Then
he

you the comforts of Chriſtianity; I requeſt them not, for I am no Chriſtian."

Infidelity,

he got diſmiſſed from his maſter and went to London, in full confidence that his literary talents would find ample employment
and encouragement from the London bookſellers; but being
diſappointed in his expectation, the fatal concluſion which has
juſt been mentioned took place. Had this been the caſe immediately on his receipt of Mr. Walpole's laſt letter, ſome ſhadow
of foundation might have appeared for the harſh cenſures
paſſed on Mr. Walpole's treatment of this ill-fated youth;
though even then, no real one, all circumſtances con-
ſidered.

From the ſpirited reply of Mr. Walpole to one of theſe
cenſurers, (the Editor of Chatterton's Miſcellanies,) and
printed in the ſame pamphlet as the letter to W. B. the
following extract is given, as equally applicable to all objectors.

" Was it the part of a juſt man to couple Chatterton's
" firſt unſucceſsful application with his fatal exit, and load
" me with both ? Does your enthuſiaſtic admiration of
" his abilities, or your regrets for the honour of England's
" poetry, warrant ſuch a concatenation of ideas ? Was
" poor Chatterton ſo modeſt, or ſo deſponding, as to aban-
" don his enterprizes on their being damped by me ? Did
" he not continue to purſue them ? Is this country ſo deſti-
" tute of patrons of genius, or do I move in ſo eminent and
" diſtinguiſhed a ſphere, that a repulſe from me is a dagger
" to talents ? Did not Chatterton come to London after
" that miſcarriage ? Did he relinquiſh his counterfeiting
" propenſity on its being loſt on me ? Was he an inoffen-

F   " ſive

Infidelity, or fcepticifm at leaft, may be termed the difeafe of young, lively, and half-informed minds. There is fomething like

" five ingenuous youth, fmit with the love of the mufes,
" and foaring above a fordid and fervile profeffion, whofe
" early bloffoms being blighted by my infolence, withered
" in mortified obfcurity, and on feeing his hopes of fame
" blafted, funk beneath the frowns of ignorant and infolent
" wealth ? or did he, after launching into all the exceffes
" you defcribe, and vainly hoping to gratify his ambition
" by adulation to, or fatires on all ranks and parties of
" men, fall a victim to his own ungovernable fpirit, and to
" the deplorable ftraits to which he had reduced himfelf?
" The interval was fhort, I own ; but as every moment of
" fo extraordinary a life was crouded with efforts of his en-
" terprifing genius, allow me to fay with truth, that there
" was a large chafm between his application to me and his
" miferable conclufion. You know there was ; and though
" my falling into his fnare might have varied the æra of
" his exploits, it is more likely that that fuccefs would
" rather have encouraged than checked his enterprifes.
" When he purfued his turn for fabricating ancient writings,
" in fpite of the mortification he received from me, it is
" not probable that he would have been corrected by fuc-
" cefs; fuch is not the nature of fuccefs, when it is the
" reward of artifice. I fhould be more juftly reproachable
" for having contributed to cherifh an impoftor, than I am
" for having accelerated his fate. I cannot repeat the
" words without emotions of indignation on my own ac-
" count, and of compaffion on his." O.

like difcovery in the rejection of truths to which they have been from infancy in trammels. A little learning, too, mifleads the underftanding, in an opinion of its own powers. When we have acquired the outlines of fcience, we are apt to fuppofe that every thing is within our comprehenfion. Much ftudy and much information are required to difcover the difficulties in which the fyftems of infidels are involved. There are profound, as well as popular arguments, in favour of revealed religion ; but when the flippancy of Voltaire or Hume has taught young perfons to fuppofe that they have defeated the former, their underftandings feldom recover fufficient vigour to purfue the latter with the ability and perfeverance of a Newton or a Bryant.

The evil effect of thefe principles upon the morals of youth, is often found to furvive the fpeculative impreffions which they

have made on the intellect.   Wretched
is that perfon, who, in the ardour and
impetuofity of youth, finds himfelf releafed from all the falutary reftraints
of duty and religion; wretched is he,
who, deprived of all the comforting
hopes of another ftate, is reduced to feek
for happinefs in the vicious gratifications
of this life; who, under fuch delufions,
acquires habits of profligacy or difcontent!
The progrefs, however, from fpeculative
to practical irreligion, is not fo rapid as is
commonly fuppofed.   The greateft advantage of a ftrict and orderly education is the
refiftance which virtuous habits, early acquired, oppofe to the allurements of vice.
Thofe who have fullied the youth of Chatterton with the imputation of extraordinary vices or irregularities, and have afferted, that " his profligacy was, at leaft, as
confpicuous as his abilities *," have, I
conceive, rather grounded thefe affertions

on

* Preface to Chatterton's Mifcellanies, p. 18.

on the apparently profane and immoral tendency of some of his productions, than on personal knowledge or a correct review of his conduct. During his residence at Briftol, we have the moft refpectable evidence in favour of the regularity of his conduct, namely, that of his mafter, Mr. Lambert. Of few young men in his fituation it can be faid, that during a courfe of nearly three years, he feldom encroached upon the ftrict limits which were affigned him, with refpect to his hours of liberty; that his mafter could never accufe him of improper behaviour, and that he had the utmoft reafon to be fatisfied he never fpent his hours of leifure in any but refpectable company.

Mrs. Newton, with that unaffected fimplicity which fo eminently characterifes her letter, moft powerfully controverts the obloquy which had been thrown upon her brother's memory. She fays, that while he was at Mr. Lambert's, he vifited

F 3   his

his mother regularly moſt evenings
before nine o'clock, and they were ſel-
dom two evenings together without ſeeing
him. He was for a conſiderable time remarkably indifferent to females. He declared to his ſiſter, that he had always ſeen
the whole ſex with perfect indifference,
except thoſe whom nature had rendered
dear. He remarked, at the ſame time,
the tendency of ſevere ſtudy to ſour the
temper, and indicated his inclination to
form an acquaintance with a young female
in the neighbourhood, apprehending that
it might ſoften that auſterity of temper
which had reſulted from ſolitary ſtudy.
The juvenile Petrarch wanted a Laura, to
poliſh his manners and exerciſe his fancy.
He addreſſed a poem to Miſs Rumſey;
and they commenced, Mrs. Newton adds,
a correſponding acquaintance. " He
would alſo frequently," ſhe ſays, " walk
the College Green with the young girls
that ſtatedly paraded there to ſhew their
finery;"

finery * ;" but she is persuaded that the reports which charge him with libertinism are ill-founded †. She could not perhaps have added a better proof of it, than his inclination to associate with modest women. The testimony of Mr. Thistlethwaite is not less explicit or less honourable to Chatterton. " The opportunities," says he, " which a long acquaintance with him

F 4   afforded

---

* In a letter from London to his sister, he particularizes ten Bristol females of his acquaintance, and adds, " I pro-" mised to write to some hundreds, I believe; but what " with writing for publications, and going to places of " public diversion, which is as absolutely necessary to me " as my food, I find but little time to write to you." O.

† Mrs. Newton's letter. I cannot help remarking a pleasant mistake of the Dean of Exeter: The orthography of Mrs. N. in the letter printed in Love and Madness, is not the most correct. Her words are, " I really believe he was no debauchee (though some have reported it) ; the dear unhappy boy had faults enough, I saw with concern ; he was proud and exceedingly imperious, but that of *venality* he could not be justly accused with." It is easy to see that Mrs. N. by *venality* means libertinism ; but the Dean taking the word in the usual sense, makes use of it to disprove, what is seldom suspected of a poet, and least of all of Chatterton, that he was avaricious.

afforded me, juftify me in faying, that
whilft he lived at Briftol, he was not the
debauched character he has been reprefented.   Temperate in his living, moderate in
his pleafures, and regular in his exercifes,
he was undeferving of the afperfion.   I
admit that amongft his papers may be
found many paffages, not only immoral,
but bordering upon a libertinifm grofs and-
unpardonable.   It is not my intention to
attempt a vindication of thofe paffages,
which, for the regard I bear his memory,
I wifh he had never written, but which I
neverthelefs believe to have originated rather from a warmth of imagination, aided
by a vain affectation of fingularity, than
from any natural depravity, or from a heart
vitiated by evil example *."

But

---

* Milles's Rowley, p. 461.   Whether the following paffage from Chatterton's Kew Gardens (a poem not publifhed
in any of the collections of his works) be received as a confirmation of his friend's teftimony in his favour, or the contrary,

But though it may not always be the
effect of infidel principles, to plunge the
perfon who becomes unfortunately infected
with them into an immediate courfe of
flagrant and fhamelefs depravity, they feldom

trary, it is, however, worth preferving. An officious
friend is introduced accofting him in the following lines :

  " Is there a ftreet within this fpacious place,
  " That boafts the happinefs of one fair face,
  " Whofe converfation does not turn on you ?
  " Blaming your wild amours, and morals too.
  " Oaths, facred and tremendous oaths you fwear,
  " Oaths which might fhock a L———'s foul to hear ;
  " Whilft the too tender and believing maid,
  " Remember pretty ——— is betray'd.
  " Then your religion !—oh, beware ! beware !
  " Although a Deift is no monfter here,
  " Think not the merit of a jingling fong
  " Can countenance the author's acting wrong.
  " Reform your manners, and with folemn air,
  " Hear Catcott bray, and Robins fqueak in prayer.

  " Damn'd narrow notions, notions which difgrace
  " The boafted freedom of the human race ;
  " Briftol may keep her prudent maxims ftill,
  " I fcorn her prudence, and I ever will.
  " Since all my vices magnified are here,
  " She cannot paint me worfe than I appear.
  " When raving in the lunacy of ink,
  " I catch the pen, and publifh what I think." O.

dom fail to unhinge the mind, and render
it the fport of fome paffion, unfriendly to
our happinefs and profperity. One of their
firft effects in Chatterton was to render the
idea of fuicide familiar, and to difpofe
him to think lightly of the moft facred
depofit with which man is entrufted by
his Creator. It has been fuppofed that
his violent death in London, was the fudden or almoft inftant effect of extreme
poverty and difappointment. It appears,
however, that long before he left Briftol,
he had repeatedly intimated to the fervants
of Mr. Lambert, his intention of putting
an end to his exiftence. Mr. Lambert's
mother was particularly terrified, but fhe
was unable to perfuade her fon of the
reality of his threats, till he found by accident upon his defk a paper, entitled,
the " Laft Will and Teftament of Thomas
Chatterton *," in which he ferioufly indicated

See the Will in the Appendix to Chatterton's Mifc.

cated his defign of committing fuicide on
the following day, namely, Eafter Sunday, April 15th, 1770. The paper was
probably rather the refult of temporary
uneafinefs *, than of that fixed averfion to
his fituation which he conftantly manifefted; but with principles and paffions fuch
as Chatterton difplayed, Mr. Lambert
confidered it as no longer prudent, after
fo decifive a proof, to continue him in the
houfe; he accordingly difmiffed him immediately from his fervice, in which he
had continued two years, nine months,
and thirteen days.

If there was any fincerity in the intentions of committing fuicide, which he expreffed in the paper above alluded to, he was
diverted from it for the prefent by the gold-
en profpects with which he flattered himfelf from a new plan of life, on which he

entered

* I have been informed from good authority, that it was
occafioned by the refufal of a gentleman, whom he had occafionally complimented in his poems, to accommodate him
with a fupply of money.

entered with his ufual enthufiafm. A few
months before he left Briftol, he had written letters to feveral bookfellers in London *, " who," Mr. Thiftlethwaite fays,
" finding him of advantage to them in
their publications, were by no means
fparing of their praifes and compliments ;
adding the moft liberal promifes of affiftance and employment, fhould he choofe
to make London the place of his refidence †." To the interrogatories of this
gentleman concerning the plan of life
which he intended to purfue on his arrival
at London, his anfwer was remarkable,
and correfponds with what has been juft
related. " My firft attempt," faid he,
" fhall be in the literary way: The promifes I have received are fufficient to difpel doubt; but fhould I, contrary to my
expectation, find myfelf deceived, I will
in that cafe turn Methodift preacher: Credulity is as potent a deity as ever, and a
new

* Mrs. Newton's Letter.
† Milles's Rowley, p. 460.

new sect may easily be devised. But if that too should fail me, my last and final resource is a pistol."

Before he quitted Bristol, he had entered deeply into politics, and had embraced what was termed the patriotic party. In March 1770, he wrote a satirical poem, called " Kew Gardens," consisting of above 1300 lines. This he transmitted, in different packets, to Mr. George William Edmunds, No. 73, Shoe-lane, Printer of a patriotic newspaper. At the bottom of the first packet, which contained about 300 lines, written in Chatterton's own hand, is this postscript. " Mr. Edmunds will send the author, Thomas Chatterton, twenty of the Journals, in which the above poem (which I shall continue) shall appear, by the machine, if he thinks proper to put it in; the money shall be paid to his orders." The poem is a satire on the Princess Dowager of Wales,

Lord

Lord Bute, and their Friends in London
and Briftol, but particularly on thofe in
Briftol, who had diftinguifhed themfelves
in favour of the Miniftry. His fignature
on this occafion was DECIMUS ; but whether the poem was ever printed or not, I
have not been able to afcertain. I have
been alfo informed of another political
fatire of near 600 lines, the manufcript of
which, in Chatterton's hand-writing, is
in the poffeffion of a friend of Mr. Catcott.
It is called "The Whore of Babylon."
The fatire of this poem is alfo directed
againft the Miniftry, and, like the former,
it includes feveral of the Briftol people,
not excepting Mr. George Catcott, and
his brother the clergyman. But his party
efforts were not confined altogether to
poetry; he wrote an invective in profe
againft Bifhop Newton, alfo figned Decimus, which, I believe, appeared in fome
of the periodical publications of the times.
The

The manufcript of this letter is in Mr. Catcott's poffeffion ; but the ftyle appears much inferior to that of his profe publications pofterior to his arrival in London. To write well in profe is perhaps more the effect of art, of ftudy, and of habit, than of natural genius. The rules of metrical compofition are fewer, more fimple, and require a lefs conftant exercife of the judgment. In the infancy of focieties, as well as of individuals, therefore, the art of poetry is antecedent to thofe of rhetoric and criticifm, and arrives at perfection long before the language of profe attains that degree of ftrength, concifenefs, and harmony, which is requifite to fatisfy a delicate ear. Chatterton wrote alfo an indecent fatirical poem, called " The Exhibition," occafioned by the improper behaviour of a perfon in Briftol. The fatire of this poem is chiefly local, and the characters of moft of the furgeons in Brif-

tol

are delineated in it.   Some defcriptive
paffages in this poem have great merit.
Thus, fpeaking of a favourite organift,
probably Mr. Allen, he fays :

" He keeps the paffions with the found in play,
" And the foul trembles with the trembling key *."

There are a number of other unpublifh-
ed works of his difperfed in the hands of
different perfons.   The activity of his
mind is indeed almoft unparalleled.   But
our furprife muft decreafe, when we confider that he flept but little; and that his
whole attention was directed to literary
purfuits; for he declares himfelf fo ignorant of his profeffion, that he was unable
to draw out a clearance from his appren-
ticefhip, which Mr. Lambert demanded †.
He was alfo unfettered by the ftudy of the
dead languages, which ufually abforb much
of

* Love and Madnefs, p. 167.

† See the third letter of Chatterton, publifhed in Lové
and Madnefs, p. 198.

of the time and attention of young perfons ; and though they may be ufeful to
the attainment of correctnefs, perhaps
they do not much contribute to fluency in
writing. Mr. Catcott declared, that when
he firft knew Chatterton, he was ignorant
even of Grammar *.

There are three great æras in the life of
Chatterton, his admiffion into Colfton's
fchool, his being put apprentice to Mr.
Lambert, and his expedition to London.
In the latter end of April, 1770, he bade
his native city (from which he had never
previoufly been abfent further than he
could walk in half a Sunday) *a final
adieu* †.   In a letter to his mother, dated
April 26th, he defcribes in a lively ftyle
the little adventures of his journey, and
his reception from his patrons, the bookfellers and printers with whom he had
                    G   cor-

* From the information of Mr. Seward.
† Love and Madnefs, p. 191.

corresponded; these were Mr. Edmunds, whom I lately had occasion to mention as a noted patriotic printer at that period; Mr. Fell, publisher of the Freeholder's Magazine; Mr. Hamilton, proprietor of the Town and Country; and Mr. Dodsley, of Pall-Mall. From all of them he professes to have received great encouragement, adding, that all approved of his design, and that he should probably be soon settled. In the same letter, he desires his mother to call upon Mr. Lambert. "Shew him this," says he, with uncommon dignity and spirit, "or tell him, if I deserve a recommendation, he would oblige me to give me one—if I do not, it would be beneath him to take notice of me *."

His first habitation after his arrival in London was at Mr. Walmsley's, a plaisterer in Shoreditch, to whom he was introduced by a relation of his, a Mrs. Ballance, who

* Love and Madness, p. 192.

who refided in the fame houfe. Of his firft eftablifhment, his report is favourable. " I am fettled," fays he, in a letter to his mother, dated May 6th, " and in fuch a fettlement as I could defire. I get four guineas a month by one magazine; fhall engage to write a hiftory of England, and other pieces, which will more than double that fum. Occafional effays for the daily papers would more than fupport me. What a glorious profpect * !" In confequence of his engagements with the different magazines, we find him, about the fame time, foliciting communications from his poetical and literary friends at Briftol, and defiring them to read the Freeholder's Magazine. In a letter dated the 14th of the fame month, he writes in the fame high flow of fpirits: He fpeaks of the great encouragement which genius meets with in London; adding, with exultation,

G 2 " If

* Love and Madnefs, p. 197.

" If Rowley had been a Londoner inſtead
of a Briſtowyan, I might have lived by
copying his works. *" He exhorts his ſiſter
to " improve in copying muſic, drawing,
and every thing which requires genius ;"
obſerving that although, " in Briſtol's
mercantile ſtyle, thoſe things may be uſe-
leſs, if not a detriment to her ; *here*
they are very profitable †. " His engagements at that period indeed appear to
have been numerous ; for beſides his employment in the magazines, he ſpeaks of
a connection which he had formed with
a doctor in muſic, to write ſongs for Ranelagh, Vauxhall, &c. ; and in a letter
of the 30th to his ſiſter, he mentions
another with a Scottiſh bookſeller, to com-
pile a voluminous hiſtory of London, to
appear in numbers, for which he was to
have

---

* Yet it does not appear that any of Rowley's pieces were
exhibited after C. left Briſtol. O.

† Love and Madneſs, p. 201.

have his board at the bookſeller's houſe, and a handſome premium *.

Party writing, however, ſeems to have been one of his favourite employments. It was agreeable to the ſatirical turn of his diſpoſition, and it gratified his vanity, by the proſpect of elevating him into immediate notice. When his relation, Mrs. Ballance, recommended it to him to endeavour to get into ſome office, he ſtormed like a madman, and alarmed the good old' lady in no inconſiderable degree, by telling her, "he hoped, with the bleſſing of God, very ſoon to be ſent priſoner to the Tower, which would make his fortune." In his ſecond letter to his mother from London, he ſays, "Mr. Wilkes knew me by my writings, ſince I firſt

G 3   cor-

---

* Love and Madneſs, p. 202. The Editor of Chatterton's Miſcellanies confounds this with Northook's Hiſtory of London; but that gentleman, in a letter printed in the St. James's Chronicle, denies having ever had the leaſt knowledge of C. Indeed the ſcheme above alluded to appears not to have been proceeded in.

corresponded with the booksellers here.
I shall visit him next week, and by his interest will insure Mrs. Ballance the Trinity House. He affirmed that what Mr.
Fell had of mine could not be the writings
of a youth, and expressed a desire to know
the author. By means of another bookseller, I shall be introduced to Townshend
and Sawbridge. I am quite familiar at the
Chapter Coffee-house, and know all the
geniusses there. A character is now unnecessary ; an author carries his character
in his pen *." He informs his sister that,
if money flowed as fast upon him as honours, he would give her a portion of five
thousand pounds. This extraordinary elevation of spirits arose from an introduction
to the celebrated patriotic Lord Mayor,
W. Beckford. Chatterton had, it seems,
addressed an essay to him, which was so
well received, that it encouraged him to

wait

* Love and Madness, p. 194.

upon his Lordſhip, in order to obtain his approbation to addreſs a ſecond letter to him,
on the ſubject of the city remonſtrance,
and its reception. " His Lordſhip (adds
he) received me as politely as a citizen
could, and warmly invited me to call on
him again. The reſt is a ſecret." His
inclination doubtleſs led him to eſpouſe
the party of oppoſition ; but he complains,
that " no money is to be got on that ſide
the queſtion ; intereſt is on the other ſide.
But he is a poor author who cannot write
on both ſides. I believe I may be introduced (and if I am not, I'll introduce myſelf) to a ruling power in the Court
party *." When Beckford died, he is ſaid
to have been almoſt frantic †, and to have
exclaimed, that he was ruined. The elegy,
however, in which he has celebrated him ‡,
G 4 contains

* Love and Madneſs, p. 203.
† Ibid. p. 214.
‡ Chat. Miſcel. p. 76.

contains more of frigid praife, than of ardent feeling; nor is there in it a fingle line which appears to flow from the heart. Indeed, that he was ferious in his intention of writing on both fides, is evident from a lift of pieces written by Chatterton, but never publifhed, which Mr. Walpole has preferved. No. V. of thefe pieces is a letter to Lord North, dated May 26th, 1770, figned *Moderator*, and beginning, " My Lord, It gives me a painful pleafure, &c." It contains, as Mr. Walpole informs us, an encomium on Adminiftration for rejecting the City Remonftrance. On the other hand, No. VI. is a letter to the Lord Mayor, Beckford, (probably that which he defired his permiffion to addrefs to him). It is alfo dated May 26, figned *Probus*, and contains a virulent invective againft Government for rejecting the Remonftrance, beginning, " When the endeavours of a fpirited people to free themfelves

felves from infupportable flavery, &c." On
the back of this eflay, which is directed
to Mr. Cary, a particular friend of Chatterton in Briftol, is this indorfement:
" Accepted by Bingley—fet for, and
thrown out of the North Briton, 21ft
June, on account of the Lord Mayor's
death.

Loft by his death on this Eſſay,		£. 1	11	6
Gained in Elegies,	£. 2 2 0			
——— In Eſſays,	3 3 0			
		5	5	0
Am glad he is dead by —		£. 3	13	6*"

" Eſſays," again ſays he to his ſiſter,
" on the patriotic ſide, fetch no more than
what the copy is fold for. As the patriots
themfelves are fearching for a place, they
have no gratuities to fpare. On the other
hand, unpopular eflays will not even be
accepted, and you muft pay to have them
printed;

Two letters printed at Strawberry-hill.

printed; but then you feldom lofe by it.
Courtiers are fo fenfible of their deficiency
in merit, that they generally reward all
who know how to daub them with an
appearance of it *." Either Chatterton,
on this occafion, fpoke from hear-fay, or
there is reafon to believe that the minif-
terial arrangements are greatly altered in
this refpect, and that moft of the late ad-
miniftrations have found a more effectual,
if a more expenfive fupport, from a venal
majority in the Houfe, than from a venal
phalanx of mendicant authors in the daily
papers.

On this fandy foundation of party writing Chatterton erected a vifionary fabric of
future greatnefs; and, in the waking dreams
of a poetical imagination, he was already
a man of confiderable public importance.
It was a common affertion with him,
" that he would fettle the nation before he
had

* Love and Madnefs, p. 204.

had done *." In a letter to his fifter of the 20th July, he tells her, "My company is courted every where ; and, could I humble myfelf to go into a compter, could have had twenty places before now; but I muft be among the great ; ftate matters fuit me better than commercial †." In a former letter he intimates, that he " might have had a recommendation to Sir George Cole-brooke, an Eaft-India Director, as quali-fied for an office no ways defpicable, but," he adds, " I fhail not take a ftep to the fea, whilft I can continue on land ‡." His tafte for diffipation feems to have kept pace with the increafe of his vanity. To frequent places of public amufement, he accounts as neceffary to him as food. " I employ my money," fays he, " now in fitting myfelf fafhionably, and getting

into

* Love and Madnefs, p. 214.
† Ibid. p. 210.
‡ Ibid. p. 203.
|| Ibid. p. 200.

into good company; this laft article always
brings me in intereft *."

While engaged in the examination of
thefe curious letters, it is impoffible not
to be attracted by a remarkable paffage.
Chatterton informs his mother in the letter of May 14th, " A gentleman, who
knows me at the Chapter, as an author,
would have introduced me as a companion
to the young Duke of Northumberland,
in his intended general tour; but, alas!
I fpeak no tongue but my own †." It is
not very credible, that any of the conftant
frequenters of the Chapter Coffee-houfe
fhould be poffeffed of influence fufficient
to recommend a perfon to the Duke of
Northumberland, to fo important an office
as that of the care of his fon; much lefs
credible is it, that fuch a perfon would
recommend a young literary adventurer,
whofe

* Love and Madnefs, p. 202.
† Ibid. p. 198.

whofe character was only known by an accidental meeting at a coffee-houfe; and leaft credible of all it is, that fuch a perfon was likely to be accepted on fo flender a ground of recommendation. It is no unfrequent fport with little minds to play with the fanguine tempers and expectations of young and unexperienced minds: Poor Chatterton had tolerable experience of thefe prodigal promifers, from the patriotic Beckford to his pretended patron at the Chapter Coffee-houfe.

The fplendid vifions of promotion and confequence however foon vanifhed, and our adventurer found no patrons but the bookfellers; and even here he feems not to have efcaped the poignant fting of difappointment. Soon after his arrival in London, he writes to his mother, " The poverty of authors is a common obfervation, but not always a true one. No author can be poor who underftands the

arts

arts of bookfellers ; without this neceffary knowledge the greateft genius may ftarve, and with it the greateft dunce may live in fplendour. This knowledge I have pretty well dipped into *." This knowledge, however, inftead of conducting to opulence and independence, proved a delufive guide; and though he boafts of having pieces in the month of June 1770 in the Gofpel Magazine, the Town and Country, the Court and City, the London, the Political Regifter, &c. and that almoft the whole Town and Country for the following month was his †, yet it appears, fo fcanty is the remuneration for thofe periodical labours, that even thefe uncommon exertions of induftry and genius were infufficient to ward off the approach of poverty; and he feems to have funk almoft at once from the higheft elevation of hope and illufion,

to

* Love and Madnefs, p. 195.
† Ibid. p. 210.

to the depths of defpair. Early in July
he removed his lodgings from Shoreditch
to Mrs. Angel's, a fack-maker in Brook-
ftreet, Holborn. Mr. Walmfley's family
affirmed that he affigned no reafon for
quitting their houfe. The author of Love
and Madnefs attributes the change to the
neceffity he was under, from the nature of
his employments, of frequenting public
places *. Is it not probable that he
might remove, left his friends in Shoreditch, who had heard his frequent boafts,
and obferved his dream of greatnefs, fhould
be the fpectators of his approaching indigence? Pride was the ruling paffion of
Chatterton, and a too acute fenfe of fhame
is ever found to accompany literary pride.
But however he might be defirous of preferving appearances to the world, he was
fufficiently lowered in his own expectations; and great indeed muft have been
his

* Love and Madnefs, p. 189.

his humiliation, when we find his tower‑
ing ambition reduced to the miferable hope
of fecuring the very ineligible appointment
of a furgeon's mate to Africa. To his
friend Mr. Barrett he applied in his dif‑
trefs for a recommendation to this un‑
promifing ftation. Even in this dreary
profpect he was not, however, without
the confolations of his mufe; his fancy
delighted itfelf with the expectation of
contemplating the wonders of a country,
where " Nature flourifhes in her moft
perfect vigour; where the *purple* aloe,
and the fcarlet jeffamine, diffufe their rich
perfumes; where the reeking tygers bafk
in the fedges, or wanton with their fhadows
in the ftream."*

His refolution was announced in a poem
to Mifs Bufh,† in the ftyle of Cowley, that
is, with too much affectation of wit for real
feeling.

* See the African Eclogues, Chat. Mif. p. 56—61.
† Chat. Mifc. p. 85.

feeling. Probably, indeed, when he compofed the African Eclogues, which was
juft before, he might not be without a
diftant contemplation of a fimilar defign;
and perhaps we are to attribute a part of
the exulting expreffions, which occur in
the letters to his mother and fifter, to the
kind and laudable intention of making
them happy with refpect to his profpects in life; fince we find him, almoft
at the very crifis of his diftrefs, fending a
number of little unneceffary prefents to
them and his grandmother, while perhaps
he was himfelf almoft in want of the ne-
ceffaries of life.

On the fcore of incapacity probably,
Mr. Barrett refufed him the neceffary recommendation, and his laft hope was blafted*. Of Mrs. Angel, with whom he

H laft

* This circumftance reflects no difgrace, but rather honour upon Mr. B. as he could not poffibly forefee the melancholy confequence, and he could not in confcience be the
inftrument

laft refided, no enquiries have afforded
any fatisfactory intelligence; but there
can be little doubt that his death was pre-
ceded by extreme indigence. Mr. Crofs,
an apothecary in Brook-ftreet, informed
Mr. Warton, that while Chatterton lived
in the neighbourhood, he frequently called
at the fhop, and was repeatedly preffed by
Mr. Crofs to dine or fup with him in vain.
One evening, however, human frailty fo
far prevailed over his dignity, as to tempt
him to partake of the regale of a bar-
rel of oyfters, when he was obferved to
eat moft voracioufly †. Mrs. Wolfe, a
barber's wife, within a few doors of the
houfe where Mrs. Angel lived, has alfo
afforded ample teftimony, both to his poverty and his pride. She fays, " that
Mrs. Angel told her, after his death, that
on the 24th of Auguft, as fhe knew he
had

inftrument of committing the lives of a confiderable number
of perfons to one totally inadequate to the charge.

    † Warton's Inquiry, p. 107.

had not eaten any thing for two or three days, fhe begged he would take fome dinner with her; but he was offended at her expreffions, which feemed to hint he was in want, and affured her he was not hungry*." In thefe defperate circumftances, his mind reverted to what (we learn from Mr. Thiftlethwaite, and other quarters) he had accuftomed himfelf to regard as a laft refource.—" Over his death, for the fake of the world," fays the author of Love and Madnefs, " I would willingly draw a veil. But this muft not be. They who are in a condition to patronife merit, and they who feel a confcioufnefs of merit which is not patronifed, may form their own refolutions from the cataftrophe of his tale;—thofe, to lofe no opportunity of befriending genius; thefe, to feize every opportunity of befriending themfelves, and, upon no account, to

H 2　　　　harbour

* Love and Madnefs, p. 219.

harbour the moſt diſtant idea of quitting
the world, however it may be unworthy
of them, leſt deſpondency ſhould at laſt
deceive them into ſo unpardonable a ſtep.
Chatterton, as appears by the Coroner's
Inqueſt, ſwallowed arſenick in water, on
the 24th of Auguſt 1770, and died in con-
ſequence thereof the next day.   He was
buried in a ſhell, in the burying ground
of Shoe-lane work-houſe *."   Whatever
unfiniſhed pieces he might have, he cautiouſly deſtroyed them before his death;
and his room, when broken open, was
found covered with little ſcraps of paper †.   What muſt increaſe our regret
for this haſty and unhappy ſtep, is the information that the late Dr. Fry, head of
St. John's College in Oxford, went to
Briſtol in the latter end of Auguſt 1770,
in order to ſearch into the hiſtory of Rowley and Chatterton, and to patroniſe the
latter,

* Love and Madneſs, p. 221.
† Ibid. p. 222.

latter, if he appeared to deferve affiftance—
when, alas ! all the intelligence he could
procure was, that Chatterton had, within
a few days, deftroyed himfelf *.

I have been induced, from the circumftances of the narrative, repeatedly to confider the character of Chatterton in the
different ftages of life in which I had occafion to contemplate him. Indeed, the
character of any man is better underftood
from a fair and accurate ftatement of his
life and conduct, than from the comments
of any critic or biographer whatever. A
few general obfervations, which could not
with fo much propriety be introduced into
the body of the narrative, 1 fhall, however, venture to fubjoin ; though I flatter
myfelf the reader is not at this time unac-
quainted with the outline of his moral portrait.

The perfon of Chatterton, like his
genius, was premature; he had a man-

H 3

lineſs

* Love and Madnefs, p. 226.

linefs and dignity beyond his years, and
there was a fomething about him uncommonly prepoffeffing. His moft remarkable feature was his eyes, which,
though gray, were uncommonly pierc-
ing ; when he was warmed in argument,
or otherwife, they fparked with fire, and
one eye, it is faid, was ftill more remarkable than the other *. His genius
will be moft completely eftimated from his
writings. He had an uncommon ardour
in the purfuit of knowledge, and uncommon facility in the attainment of it. It
was a favourite maxim with him, that
" man is equal to any thing, and that
every thing might be atchieved by diligence and abftinence †." His imagination,

* Love and Madnefs, p. 27!.

† Ibid. p. 183. If any uncommon charaƈer was mentioned in his hearing, " All boy as he was, he would only
obferve, that the perfon in queftion merited praife ; but
that God had fent his creatures into the world with arms
long enough to reach any thing, if they would be at the
trouble of extending them." Ib.

tion, like Dryden's, was more fertile than
correct; and he seems to have erred rather
through hafte and negligence, than through
any deficiency of tafte. He was above that
puerile affectation which pretends to borrow nothing; he knew that original genius
confifts in forming new and happy combinations, rather than in fearching after
thoughts and ideas which never had oc-
curred before; and that the man who
never imitated, has feldom acquired a habit
of good writing. If thofe poems, which
pafs under the name of Rowley, be really
the productions of Chatterton, he poffeffed
the ftrongeft marks of a vigorous imagination and a found judgment, in forming
great, confiftent, and ingenious plots, and
making choice of the moft interefting fubjects. If Rowley and Chatterton be the
fame, it will be difficult to fay whether he
excelled moft in the fublime or the fatirical; and as a univerfal genius, he muft rank

H 4

above

above Dryden, and perhaps only ftand fecond to Shakefpeare. If, on the other hand,
we are to judge altogether from thofe pieces
which are confeffedly his own, we muft
undoubtedly affign the preference to thofe
of the fatirical clafs.   In moft of his ferious writings, there is little that indicates
their being compofed with a full relifh ;
when he is fatirical, his foul glows in his
compofition.

Mr. Catcott affirms that Chatterton underftood   no   language   but   his   mother
tongue ; the fame fact feems to be implied
in his own confeffion, " that he fpoke no
tongue but his own *;" and it receives decifive confirmation from the teftimony of
Mr. Smith, in his converfation with Dr.
Glynn ; yet we find him, even fo early
as the year 1768, annexing a Latin fignature to the " Accounte of the Fryers
paffing

* Love and Madnefs, p. 198.

paffing the old Bridge," and there are fome attempts at infcriptions in old French, in the defign which he planned for his own tomb-ftone * He, probably, might have acquired fome little knowledge of both thefe languages; but even if this were the cafe, there can be no doubt that it was very fuperficial. When we confider the variety of his engagements while at Briftol, his extenfive reading, and the great knowledge he had acquired of the ancient language of his native country, we cannot wonder that he had not time to occupy himfelf in the ftudy of other languages; and after his arrival in London, he had a new and neceffary fcience to learn, the world; and that he made the moft advantageous ufe of his time is evident from the extenfive knowledge of mankind difplayed in the different effays, which he produced occafionally for periodical publications.

* Chatterton's Will, in App. to Mifc.

cations. The lively and vigorous imági-
nation of Chatterton contributed, doubtlefs, to animate him with that fpirit of
enterprife, which led him to form fo many
impracticable and vifionary fchemes, for
the acquifition of fame and fortune. His
ambition was evident from his earlieft
youth; and perhaps the inequality of his
fpirits might, in a great meafure, depend
upon the fairnefs of his views, or the diffipation of his projects. His melancholy
was extreme on fome occafions, and, at
thofe times, he conftantly argued in favour of fuicide. Mr. Catcott left him one
evening totally depreffed; but he returned
the next morning with unufual fpirits.
He faid, " he had fprung a mine," and
produced a parchment, containing the
Sprytes, a poem, now in the poffeffion of
Mr. Barrett *.

His

* From the information of Mr. Seward.

His natural melancholy was not corrected by the irreligious principles, which he
had fo unfortunately imbibed. To thefe
we are certainly to attribute his premature
death; and, if he can be proved guilty of
the licentioufnefs which is by fome laid to
his charge, it is reafonable to believe that
a fyftem, which exonerates the mind from
the apprehenfion of future punifhment,
would not contribute much to reftrain the
criminal exceffes of the paffions. Had
Chatterton lived, and been fortunate enough
to fall into fettled and fober habits of life,
his excellent underftanding would, in all
probability, have led him to fee the fallacy
of thofe principles, which he had haftily
embraced; as it was, the only prefterva-
tives of which he was poffeffed againft the
contagion of vice, were the enthufiafm of
literature, and that delicacy of fentiment
which tafte and reading infpire. But
though thefe auxiliaries are not wholly to

be

despised, we have too many instances of their inefficacy in supporting the cause of virtue, to place any confident reliance on them.

Under such circumstances there is little cause for surprize, if the passions of Chatterton should frequently have trespassed the boundaries of reason and moral duty. That he had strong resentments is evident from his great disposition to satire, and particularly from the letter which has been mentioned as written by him to his schoolmaster, soon after the commencement of his apprenticeship. That he was " proud and imperious," is allowed by his sister, and the generality of his acquaintance. He stands charged with a profligate attachment to women; the accusation, however, is stated in a vague and desultory manner, as if from common report, without any direct or decided evidence in support of the opinion. To the regularity

rity of his conduct during his refidence in
Briftol, fome refpectable teftimonies have
been already exhibited. It is, indeed, by
no means improbable, that a young man
of ftrong paffions, and unprotected by religious principles, might frequently be
unprepared to refift the temptations of a
licentious metropolis; yet, even after his
arrival in London, there are fome proofs in
his favour, which ought not to be difre-
garded. During a refidence of nine weeks
at Mr. Walmfley's, he never ftaid out beyond the family hours, except one night,
when Mrs. Ballance knew that he lodged
at the houfe of a relation*.

Whatever may be the truth of thefe
reports, the lift of his virtues ftill appears
to exceed the catalogue of his faults. His
temperance was in fome refpects exem-
plary. He feldom eat animal food, and
never tafted any ftrong or fpirituous li-
quors :

* Love and Madnefs, p. 261.

quors: he lived chiefly on a morfel of bread or a tart, with a draught of water. His fifter affirms, that he was a lover of truth from the earlieft dawn of reafon; and that his fchool-mafter depended on his veracity on all occafions *: the pride of genius will feldom defcend to the moft contemptible of vices, falfehood. His high fenfe of dignity has been already noticed in two moft ftriking inftances; but the moft amiable feature in his character, was his generofity and attachment to his mother and relations. Every favourite project for his advancement in life was accompanied with promifes and encouragement to them; while in London, he continued to fend them prefents, at a time when he was known himfelf to be in want: and indeed, the unremitting attention, kindnefs and refpect, which appear in the whole of his conduct towards them, are deferving the imitation of thofe

der

* Mrs. N's letter, ibid.

in more fortunate circumftances, and under the influence of better principles of
faith than Chatterton poffeffed *.

He had a number of friends, and notwithftanding his difpofition to fatire, he
is fcarcely known to have had any enemies. By the accounts of all who were
acquainted with him, there was fomething uncommonly infinuating in his
manner and converfation. Mr. Crofs informed Mr. Warton, that in Chatterton's frequent vifits while he refided at
Brook-ftreet, he found his converfation,
a little infidelity excepted, moft captivat-
ing †. His extenfive, though in many inftances, fuperficial knowledge, united with
his genius, wit and fluency, muft have
admirably accomplifhed him for the pleafures of fociety. His pride, which perhaps

* It can never be fufficiently lamented, that this amiable
propenfity was not more uniform in Chatterton. A real
love for his relations ought to have arrefted the hand of
fuicide ; but when religion is loft, all uniformity of prin-
ciple is loft. O.

† Warton's Inquiry, 107.

haps fhould rather be termed the ftrong
confcioufnefs of intellectual excellence,
did not deftroy his affability. He was
always acceffible, and rather forward to
make acquaintance, than apt to decline
the advances of others *. There is reafon
however to believe, that the inequality of
his fpirits, affected greatly his behaviour
in company. His fits of abfence were
frequent and long. "He would often
look ftedfaftly in a perfon's face without
fpeaking, or feeming to fee the perfon,
for a quarter of an hour or more †."

Chatterton had one ruling paffion which
governed his whole conduct, and that was
the defire of literary fame; this paffion in-
truded itfelf on every occafion, and abforbed
his whole attention. Whether he would
have

* " Laft week being in the pit of Drury Lane theatre,
" I contracted an immediate acquaintance (which you know
" is no hard tafk to me) with a young gentleman, &c.
Letter to his mother, Love and Madnefs, p. 197.

† Love and Madnefs, p. 214.

have continued to improve or the contrary, muſt have depended in ſome meaſure on the circumſtances of his future life. Had he fallen into profligate habits and connections, he would probably have loſt a great part of his ardour for the cultivation of his mind; and his maturer age would only have diminiſhed the admiration which the efforts of his childhood have ſo juſtly excited.

At the ſhrine of Chatterton, ſome grateful incenſe has been offered. Mr. Warton ſpeaks of him as "a prodigy of genius," as, " ſingular inſtance of a prematurity of abilities." He adds, that "he poſſeſſed a comprehenſion of mind, and an activity of underſtanding, which predominated over his ſituation in life, and his opportunities of inſtruction*" And Mr. Malone "believes him to have been the greateſt genius that England has pro-

I   duced

* Hiſtory of Engliſh poetry.

duced fince the days of Shakefpear *."
Mr. Croft †, the ingenious author of
Love and Madnefs, to whom in the
courfe of this work I have had many
obligations, is ftill more unqualified in his
praifes. He afferts, that " no fuch human
being, at any period of life, has ever been
known, or poffibly ever will be known."
He adds, in another place, " an army of
Macedonian and Swedifh mad butchers,
indeed, fly before him ; nor does my memory fupply me with any human being,
who, at fuch an age, with fuch difadvantages, has produced fuch compofitions ‡.

Under

* Curfory Obfervations on the Poems attributed to Rowley, p. 41.
† Editor of an intended new Englifh Dictionary.
‡ *Mohammed*, it is true, with hardly the ufual education of
his illiterate tribe, unable (as was imagined, and he pretended) even to read or write, *forged* the KORAN ; which
is to this day the moft elegant compofition in the Arabic
language, and its ftandard of excellence.   Upon the argument of improbability, that a man fo illiterate fhould compofe a book fo admired, *Mohammed* artfully refted the prin-
ciptal

Under the Heathen mythology, fuperftition and admiration would have explained all by bringing Apollo upon
earth : nor would the god ever have
defcended with more credit to himfelf."

The following parallel alfo by the
fame ingenious critic, does equal credit
to the ingenuity of its author, and the
reputation of Chatterton.

Milton enjoyed every ad-vantage not only of private, but of public, not only of domeftic, but of foreign edu-cation.	Chatterton wanted every advantage of every poffible education.
Milton	Chatterton

cipal evidence of his *Koran*'s divinity. (Sale's Koran,
P. Difcourfe, p. 42, 60.) He, who, merely from improbability, denies Chatterton to be the author of Rowley's
Poems, muft go near to admit God to be the author of the
Koran. But, before we compare together Chatterton and
Mohammed, it fhould be remembered that Mohammed was
forty when he commenced prophet. Perhaps the moft extraordinary circumftance about Mohammed is, that even
familiarity could not fink him into contempt; that he
contrived to be a hero and a prophet, even to his wives and
his *valets de chambre*. Even his fits of the epilepfy he converted into proofs of his divine miffion. It is probable,
that, if *Mohammed* had been lefs falacious, and not fubject

Milton in his youth received such instructions from teachers and schoolmasters, that, in his age, he was able to become a schoolmaster, and a teacher to others.

Milton's juvenile writings would not have justified a prophecy of Paradise Lost: but the author of them flatters himself, by dating his life 15 till he had turned 16.

Milton did not produce *Comus* much earlier than in his 26th year; since it was first presented at Ludlow in 1634, and he was born in 1608. In 1645, when he was 37, Allegro and Penseroso, first appeared. In 1655, when he was 47, after *long choosing, and beginning late,* he set himself to turn a strange thing, called a Mystery, into an epic poem; which was not completed in less than Chatterton's whole active existence, since the copy was not sold till April, 1667,

Chatterton became his own teacher and his own schoolmaster before other children are subjects for instruction; and never knew any other.

Few, if any, of Milton's juvenile writings would have been owned by Chatterton, at least by Rowley, could he have past for the author of them.

Chatterton, not suffered to be *long choosing,* or to *begin late,* in 17 years and 9 months, reckoning from his cradle to his grave, produced the volume of Rowley's poems, his volume of Miscellanies, and many things which are not printed, beside what his indignation tore in pieces the day he spurned at the world, and threw himself on the anger of his Creator.

to the falling sickness, out of thirty equal divisions of the known world, whereof Christianity claims five, and Paganism nineteen, the inhabitants of six would not now believe in the *Koran.*

1667, and then, confifted
only of 10 books. With all
its glorious perfections, Paradife Loft contains puerili-
ties, to which Chatterton
was a ftranger. In 3 years
more, when he was 62, ap-
peared Milton's Hiftory of
England. Paradife Regained,
and Sampfon, were publifhed
in the fame year. Lycidas I
had forgotten. It was written
in his 29th year. That propriety of character and fituation, which Chatterton can
feldom have violated, or he
would not to this moment
deceive fuch and fo many
men, Milton feldom pre-
ferves in Lycidas. If, in
the courfe of an exiftence
almoft four times longer
than Chatterton's, this man
*(fallen on evil days and evil
tongues,* with lefs truth than
Chatterton), who bore no
fruit worth gathering till
after the age at which Chatterton was withered by the
hand of Death—if, I fay,
this great man produced other
writings, he will not quarrel
that pofterity has forgotten
them; if he fhould, pofterity
will ftill perhaps forget them.

Milton's   I 3   What

Milton's manuscripts, preserved at Cambridge, bear testimony to his frequent and commendable correction.

Milton, as Ellwood relates, could never bear to hear Paradise Lost preferred before Paradise Regained. He is known to have pronounced Dryden to be no poet.

Milton, more from inclination than want of bread, it seems, entered into party disputes, whether a king might be lawfully beheaded, &c. with a servility and a virulence, and let out his praise to hire, perhaps, with a meanness, at all periods of his life, which the worst enemies of Chatterton cannot prove him to have equalled.

Milton, in affluence (if compared with others beside Chatterton)

What time could Chatterton have found for alteration or correction, when I maintain that any boy who should only have fairly *transcribed*, before his 18th year, all that Chatterton, before his 18th year, invented and composed, would be thought to deserve the reputation of diligence, and the praise of application?

If Chatterton, much earlier in life than Milton was calculated either to be an author or a critick, had not possessed a chaster judgment, he would not still impose on so many criticks and authors.

Chatterton, in order to procure bread for himself, a grandmother, mother and sister, was ready to prove the patriotism of Bute, or of Beckford, in writings, which older men need not blush to own, and in an age when older men did not blush at such a *profession*.

Chatterton, steeped to the lips in poverty, entertained,

long

Chatterton) felt on his brows thofe laurels which others could not fee ; and was per-fuaded that, " by labour and " intenfe ftudy, his portion " in this life, he might " leave fomething fo written " to after-times, as they " fhould not willingly let it " die."

long before he had lived 18 years, ideas, hopes, perfua-fions, *(by labour and intenfe ftudy,* more truly *bis portion in this life* than Milton's) of living to all eternity in the memory of Fame.

Paradife Loft produced the author and the widow only 28 pounds. The meaner, more fervile, and more ver-fatile abilities of the author produced him indeed enough to be deprived of four thou-fand pounds by ill-fortune, and to leave fifteen hundred pounds to his family.

Mr. Catcott and Mr. Bar-rett muft inform the world whether Rowley's poems and his own together produced Chatterton 28 fhillings.

Phillips relates of Milton, from his own mouth, that " his vein never happily " flowed but from the " autumnal equinox to " the vernal." Richardfon writes, that " his poetical " faculty would on a fub-" den rufh upon him with " an impetus or æftrum."

What is faid of Chatter-ton, and of the moon's effect, upon him, you have read.

Milton, when a man, fel-dom drank any thing ftrong: he ate with delicacy and temperance.

Chatterton, when a boy, hardly ever touched meat, and drank only water : when a child, he would often re-

Milton's hiſtorians and grand-daughter admit his moroſeneſs to his children, and that he would not let them learn to write.

fuſe to take any thing but bread and water, even if it did happen that his mother had a hot meal, " becauſe " he had a work in hand, " and he muſt not make " himſelf more ſtupid than " God had made him."
Chatterton's mother, his ſiſter and his letters, can ſpeak beſt of his heart, and of his wiſhes that his ſiſter might learn every thing.

To theſe I ſhall add the teſtimony of Mr. Knox:

" Unfortunate boy! ſhort and evil were thy days, but thy fame ſhall be immortal. Hadſt thou been known to the munificent patrons of genius—

" Unfortunate boy! poorly waſt thou accommodated during thy ſhort ſojourning among us;—rudely waſt thou treated,—ſorely did thy feeling ſoul ſuffer from the ſcorn of the unworthy; and there are, at laſt,

laſt, thoſe who wiſh to rob thee of thy
only meed, thy poſthumous glory. Se-
vere too are the cenſurers of thy morals.
In the gloomy moments of deſpondency,
I fear thou haſt uttered impious and blaſ-
phemous thoughts, which none can defend, and which neither thy youth, nor
thy fiery ſpirit, nor thy ſituation, can ex-
cuſe. But let thy more rigid cenſors reflect, that thou waſt literally and ſtrictly
but a boy. Let many of thy bittereſt
enemies reflect what were their own religious principles, and whether they had
any, at the age of fourteen, fifteen, and
ſixteen. Surely it is a ſevere and an un-
juſt ſurmiſe, that thou wouldeſt probably
have ended thy life as a victim of the
laws, if thou hadſt not finiſhed it as thou
didſt; ſince the very act by which thou
durſt put an end to thy painful exiſtence,
proves that thou thoughteſt it better to
die,

die, than to fupport life by theft or violence.

" The fpeatulative errors of a boy who
wrote from the fudden fuggeftions of paffion or defpondency, who is not convicted
of any immoral or difhoneft act in confequence of his fpeculations, ought to be
configned to oblivion. But there feems
to be a general and inveterate diflike to
the boy, exclufively of the poet; a diflike which many will be ready to impute,
and, indeed, not without the appearance
of reafon, to that infolence and envy of
the little great, which cannot bear to ac-
knowledge fo tranfcendent and command-
ing a fuperiority in the humble child of
want and obfcurity.

" Malice, if there was any, may furely
now be at reft; for " Cold he lies in the
grave below." But where were ye, O ye
friends to genius, when, ftung with difappointment,

appointment, diftreffed for food and rai-
ment, with every frightful form of human mifery painted on his fine imagination, poor Chatterton funk in defpair?
Alas! ye knew him not then, and now it
is to late,—

> For now he is dead;
> Gone to his death bed,
> All under the willow tree.

So fang the fweet youth, in as tender
an elegy as ever flowed from a feeling
heart.

" In return for the pleafure I have received from thy poems, I pay thee, poor
boy, the trifling tribute of my praife.
Thyfelf thou haft emblazoned; thine
own monument thou haft erected: But
they whom thou haft delighted, feel a
pleafure in vindicating thine honours
from the rude attacks of detrac-
tion *".

The

* Knox's Effays, No. 144.

The poetic eulogiums have, however, exceeded, both in number and excellence, the compliments of critical writers; a few remarkably interefting and beautiful, I fhall felect, with the double view of adorning the work, and gratifying the reader.

A poet, whofe fuperior elegance and claffical tafte do not appear to have met with all the applaufe they have deferved, thus fpeaks of Chatterton :

> " Yet as with ftreaming eye the forrowing mufe,
> " Pale CHATTERTON's untimely urn bedews;
> " Her accents fhall arraign the partial care,
> " That fhielded not her fon from cold defpair * .

There is a beautiful monody written by Mrs. Cowley, inferted in the laft edition of Love and Madnefs.—It is as follows :

> O CHATTERTON! for thee the penfive fong I raife,
> Thou object of my wonder, pity, envy, praife!
> Bright Star of Genius!—torn from life and fame,
> My tears, my verfe, fhall confecrate thy name!

Ye

* Pye's Progrefs of Refinement, Part 2.

Ye Mufes! who around his natal bed
Triumphant fung, and all your influence fhed;
APOLLO! thou who rapt his infant breaft,
And in his dædal numbers fhone confeft,
Ah! why, in vain, fuch mighty gifts beftow?
—Why give frefh tortures to the Child of Woe?
Why thus, with barb'rous care, illume his mind,
Adding new fenfe to all the ills behind?

    Thou haggard Poverty! whofe cheerlefs eye
Transforms young Rapture to the pond'rous figh,
In whofe drear cave no Mufe e'er ftruck the lyre,
Nor Bard e'er madden'd with poetic fire;
Why all thy fpells for CHATTERTON combine?
His thought creative, why muft thou confine?
Subdu'd by thee, his pen no more obeys,
No longer gives the fong of ancient days;
Nor paints in glowing tints from diftant fkies,
Nor bids wild fcen'ry rufh upon our eyes——
Check'd in her flight, his rapid Genius cowers,
Drops her fad plumes, and yields to thee her powers.

    Behold him, Mufes! fee your fav'rite fon
The prey of want, ere manhood is begun!
The bofom ye have fill'd, with anguifh torn——
The mind you cherifh'd, drooping and forlorn!

    And now Defpair her fable form extends,
Creeps to his couch, and o'er his pillow bends.
Ah, fee! a deadly bowl the fiend conceal'd,
Which to his eye with caution is reveal'd——
Seize it, Apollo!—feize the liquid fnare!
Dafh it to earth, or diffipate in air!
Stay, haplefs Youth! refrain—abhor the draught,
With pangs, with racks, with deep repentance fraught!

                             Oh,

Oh, hold! the cup with woe ETERNAL flows,
More—more than Death the pois'nous juice beftows!
In vain!—he drinks—and now the fearching fires
Rufh through his veins, and writhing he expires!
No forrowing friend, no fifter, parent, nigh,
To footh his pangs, or catch his parting figh;
Alone, unknown, the Mufe's darling dies,
And with the vulgar dead unnoted lies!
Bright Star of Genius!—torn from life and fame
My tears, my verfe, fhall confecrate thy name!

Nor has the Mufe of Amwell been
backward in commendation.

And BRISTOL! why thy fcenes explore,
  And why thofe fcenes fo foon refign,
And fail to feek the fpot that bore
  That wonderous tuneful Youth of thine,
The Bard, whofe boafted ancient ftore
Rofe recent from his own exhauftlefs mine † !

Though Fortune all her gifts denied,
  Though Learning made him not her choice,
The Mufe ftill placed him at her fide,
  And bade him in her fmile rejoice—
Defcription ftill his pen fupplied,
Pathos his thought, and Melody his voice!

Confcious and proud of merit high,
  Fame's wreath he boldly claim'd to wear;

But

---

† This is at leaft the Author's opinion, notwithftanding all that has
hitherto appeared on the other fide of the queftion. The laft line
alludes to one of the ingenious Mr. Mafon in his Elegy to a young
Nobleman:
  " See from the depths of his exhauftlefs mine
  " His glittering ftores the tuneful fpendthrift throws."

But Fame, regardlefs, pafs'd him by,
    Unknown, or deem'd unworth her care :
The Sun of Hope forfook his fky ;
And all his land look'd dreary, bleak, and bare !

Then Poverty, grim fpectre, rofe,
    And horror o'er the profpect threw—
His deep diftrefs too nice to expofe ;
    Too nice for common aid to fue,
A dire alternative he chofe,
And rafhly from the painful fcene withdrew.

Ah! why for Genius' headftrong rage
    Did Virtue's hand no curb prepare ?
What boots, poor youth ! that now thy page
    Can boaft the public praife to fhare,
The learn'd in deep refearch engage,
And lightly entertain the gentle fair ?

Ye, who fuperfluous wealth command,
    O why your kind relief delay'd ?
O why not fnatch'd his defperate hand ?
    His foot on Fate's dread brink not ftay'd ?
What thanks had you your native land
For a new SHAKESPEARE or new MILTON paid !

For me—Imagination's power
    Leads oft infenfibly my way,
To where, at midnight's filent hour,
    The crefcent moon's flow-weftering ray
Pours full on REDCLIFF's lofty tower,
And gilds with yellow light its walls of grey.

'Midft Toil and Commerce flumbering round,
    Lull'd by the rifing tide's hoarfe roar,
There Frome and Avon willow-crown'd,
    I view fad-wandering by the fhore,

With

With ftreaming tears, and notes of mournful found,
Too late their haplefs Bard, untimely loft, deplore.

The following lines are uncommonly
animated and poetical :

If changing times fuggeft the pleafing hope,
That Bards no more with adverfe fortune cope;
That in this alter'd clime, where Arts increafe,
And make our polifh'd Ifle a fecond Greece;
That now, if Poefy proclaims her Son,
And challenges the wreath by Fancy won;
Both Fame and Wealth adopt him as their heir,
And liberal Grandeur makes his life her care;
From fuch vain thoughts thy erring mind defend,
And look on CHATTERTON's difaftrous end.
Oh, ill-ftarr'd Youth, whom Nature form'd in vain,
With powers on Pindus' fplendid height to reign!
O dread example of what pangs await
Young Genius ftruggling with malignant fate!
What could the Mufe, who fir'd thy infant frame
With the rich promife of Poetic fame;
Who taught thy hand its magic art to hide,
And mock the infolence of Critic pride;
What cou'd her unavailing cares oppofe,
To fave her darling from his defperate foes;
From preffing Want's calamitous controul,
And Pride, the fever of the ardent foul?
Ah, fee, too confcious of her failing power,
She quits her Nurfling in his deathful hour!
In a chill room, within whofe wretched wall
No cheering voice replies to Mifery's ca1;
Near a vile bed, too crazy to fuftain
Misfortune's wafted limbs, convuls'd with pain,

Or

On the bare floor, with heaven-directed eyes,
The haplefs Youth in fpeechlefs horror lies!
The pois'nous phial, by diftraction drain'd,
Rolls from his hand, in wild contortion ftrain'd:
Pale with life-wafting pangs, it's dire effect,
And ftung to madnefs by the world's neglect,
He, in abhorrence of the dangerous Art,
Once the dear idol of his glowing heart,
Tears from his Harp the vain detefted wires,
And in the frenzy of Defpair expires* !

Again, with all the honeft refentment of
indignant Genius,

Search the dark fcenes were drooping Genius lies,
And keep from forrieft fights a nation's eyes,
That, from expiring Want's reproaches free,
Our generous country ne'er may weep to fee
A future CHATTERTON by poifon dead,
An OTWAY fainting for a little bread†.

To thefe elegant offerings to the genius
of Chatterton, it is with peculiar pleafure I add a fonnet to expreffion, from the
polifhed and pathetic pen of Mifs Helen
Maria Williams.

Expreffion, child of foul! I fondly trace
Thy ftrong enchantments, when the poet's lyre,
The painter's pencil catch thy facred fire,
And beauty wakes for thee her touching grace—
But from this frighted glance thy form avert
When horrors check thy tear, thy ftruggling figh,
When frenzy rolls in thy impaffion'd eye,
Or guilt fits heavy on thy lab'ring heart—

K   Nor

* Hayley's Effay on Epic Poetry, Ep. iv. l. 211 to 248.
† Ibid, 336 to 342.

Nor ever let my fhudd'ring fancy bear
 The wafting groan, or view the pallid look
 Of him * the Mufes lov'd—when hope forfook
His fpirit, vainly to the Mufes dear!
For charm'd with heav'nly fong, this bleeding breaft,
Mourns the bleft power of verfe could give defpair no
  reft.—

Independent of the poems attributed to
Rowley, Chatterton has left behind him
a variety of pieces, publifhed and unpub-
lifhed; the moft confiderable of the former are to be found in a volume of mifcellanies, publifhed in 1778, to which is
prefixed a fketch for the late Alderman
Beckford's ftatue, a fpecimen of Chatterton's abilities in the arts of drawing and
defign; and this publication was followed
in 1786, by " a fuppliment to the mifcellanies of Thomas Chatterton." The compofitions contained in both thefe volumes
are fcarcely to be infpected with all the
feverity of criticifm. Confiderable allow-
ances ought to be made for the exercifes

of

* Chatterton.

of his infantine years, for the incorrect
effufions of momentary refentment, for a
few lines thrown together in a playful
mood to pleafe an illiterate female, or to
amufe a fchool-fellow, and perhaps not
lefs for the hafty and involuntary productions of indigence and neceffity, conftruct-
ed for a magazine, and calculated for the
fole purpofe of procuring a fubfiftence.
Of the poetical part of thefe mifcellanies,
I have already intimated, that the ferious
are inferior to the fatirical.

In the elegy to the memory of Mr.
Thomas Phillips, of Fairford, we, however, meet with fome defcriptive ftanzas,
perhaps not unworthy the author of Rowley's poems:

" Pale rugged Winter bending o'er his head,
" His grizzled hair bedropt with icy dew;
" His eyes, a dufky light, congealed and dead;
" His robe, a tinge of bright ethereal blue.
" His train a motley'd, fanguine fable cloud,
" He limps along the ruffet dreary moor;
" Whilft rifing whirlwinds, blafting, keen and loud,
" Roll the white furges to the founding fhore."
" Fancy,

" Fancy, whofe various, figure tinctured veft
" Was ever changing to a different hue ;
" Her head, with varied bays and flow'rets dreft,
" Her eyes two fpangles of the morning dew."

" Now as the mantle of the evening fwells,
" Upon my mind I feel a thick'ning gloom !
" Ah ! could I charm, by friendfhip's potent fpells,
" The foul of Philip's from the deathy tomb !
" Then would we wander thro' the dark'ned vale,
" In converfe fuch as heavenly fpirits ufe,
" And borne upon the plumage of the gale,
" Hymn the creator and exhort the Mufe *."

In a letter to his friend Cary, dated
London, July 1, 1770, Chatterton tells
him, " in the laft London magazine, and
in that which comes out to day, are the
only two pieces of mine I have the vanity
to call poetry." Thefe were the two
African Eclogues, publifhed in his Mifcellanies.   I am forry I cannot unite with
the author in the commendation of thefe
pieces ; but Chatterton, as well as Milton, feems to have been incapable of efti-
mating rightly the refpective merits of his

own

* Chatterton's Mifcellanies.

own productions *.   They are uncon-
nected and unequal, though it muft be
confeffed, that they contain fome excellent lines ; the following occur almoft at
the beginning of the firft eclogue, and are
animated, expreffive and harmonious :

" High from the ground the youthful warriors fprung,
" Loud on the concave fhell the lances rung :
" In all the myftic mazes of the dance,
" The youths of Banny's burning fands advance,
" Whilft the foft virgin, panting, looks behind,
" And rides upon the pinions of the wind †."

Of the correctnefs of the following
fimile in the fecond eclogue, I fhall not
determine; but the livelinefs of the defcription evinces a moft vigorous imagination.

" On Tiber's banks, clofe rank'd, a warring train,
" Stretch'd to the diftant edge of Galca's plain :
" So when arrived at Gaigra's higheft fteep,
" We view the wide expanfion of the deep ;
" See in the gilding of her wat'ry robe,
" The quick deelenfion of the circling globe ;
                    K 3   " From

* I know fome refpectable friends, who efteem this inftance of bad
tafte, as a ftrong prefumptive argument againft Chatterton being the author of Rowley's poems.
  † Chatterton's Mifcellanies, p. 56.

" From the blue fea a chain of mountains rife,
" Blended at once with water and with fkies :
" Beyond our fight in vaft extenfion curl'd,
" The check of waves, the guardian of the world *."

The fatire of Chatterton has more of the luxuriance, fluency, and negligence of Dryden, than of the terfenefs and refinement of Pope. The following lines are in the ftyle of the former :

" Search nature o'er, procure me, if you can,
" The fancied character, an honeft man.
" A man of fenfe not honeft by conftraint,
" (For fools are canvafs, living but in paint)
" To Mammon, or to fuperftition flaves,
" All orders of mankind are fools or knaves :
" In the firft attribute by none furpafs'd,
" * * * * endeavours to obtain the laft †."

The following is an evident imitation of Mr. Pope, even to the cadence of the verfe, but it is not equally fuccefsful with the laft fpecimen :

" But why muft Chatterton felected fit,
" The butt of every Critic's little wit ?
" Am I alone for ever in a crime,
" *Nonfenfe in profe,* or *blafphemy in rhyme ?*

" All

* Chatterton's Mifcellanies, p. 56.
† Epiftle to the Rev. Mr. Catcott, Append. to Chat. Mif. p. 23.

"All monofyllables a line appears!—
"Is it not very often fo in Shears?
"See gen'rous Eccas, length'ning out my praife,
"Inraptured with the mufic of my lays;
"In all the arts of panegyric grac'd,
"The cream of modern literary tafte*."

In a poem on Happinefs, inferted in Love and Madnefs, are fome ftrokes of fatire in a fuperior ftyle:

"Come to my pen, companion of the lay,
"And fpeak of worth, where merit ———
"Let lazy B——— undiftinguifh'd fnore,
"Nor lafh his generofity to ———,
"Praife him for fermons of his curate bought,
"His eafy flow of words, his depth of thought;
"His active fpirit ever in difplay,
"His great devotion when he drawls to pray,
"His fainted foul diftinguifhably feen,
"With all the virtues of a modern Dean†."

"Pulvis, whofe knowledge centres in degrees,
"Is never happy but when taking fees:
"Bleft with a bufhy wig and folemn pace,
"Catcott admires him for a *foffile* face."
—"Mould'ring in duft the fair Lavinia lies,
"Death and our Doctor clos'd her fparkling eyes,
"O all ye pow'rs, the guardians of the world!
"Where is the ufelefs bolt of vengeance hurl'd?

"Say

* The Defence, ibid. p. 37.
† Love and Madnefs, p. 155.

" Say, fhall this leaden fword of plague prevail,
" And kill the mighty where the mighty fail ?
" Let the red bolus tremble o'er his head,
" And with his guardian julep ftrike him dead * !"

In the volume of his mifcellanies are two political pieces, the Confuliad, written at Briftol, and in the higheft ftrain of party fcurrility †; and the Prophecy, written apparently a fhort time after, which is in the beft ftyle of Swift's mi-

nor

* Love and Madnefs, 156.

† The introduction to this poem is not deftitute of merit.
Of warring fenators, and battles dire,
Of quails uneaten ; Mufe, awake the lyre.
Where C—pb—ll's chimneys overlook the fquare,
And N—t—n's future profpects hang in air ;
Where counfellors difpute, and cockers match,
And Caledonian earls in concert fcratch ;
A group of heroes, occupied the round,
Long in the rolls of infamy renown'd,
Circling the table all in filence fat,
Now tearing bloody lean, now champing fat ;
Now picking ortolans, and chicken flain,
To form the whimfies of an *à la-reine :*
Now ftorming caftles of the neweft tafte,
And granting articles to forts of pafte :
Now fwallowing bitter draughts of Pruffian beer ;
Now fucking tallow of falubrious deer,

nor pieces, and appears to be the genuine effufion of that enthufiaftic love of liberty, which in tumultuous times generally takes poffeffion of young and fanguine difpo- fitions*. Of

* THE PROPHECY.

This truth of old was forrow's friend,
" Times at the worft will furely mend."
The difficulty's then to know,
How long oppreffion's clock can go;
When Britain's fons may ceafe to figh,
And hope that their redemption's nigh.

When Vice exalted takes the lead,
And Vengeance hangs but by a thread;
Gay peereffes turn'd out o'doors;
Whoremafters peers, and fons of whores;
Look up, ye Britons! ceafe to figh,
For your redemption draweth nigh.

When vile Corruption's brazen face,
At council-board fhall take her place;
And lords-commiffioners refort,
To welcome her at Britain's court;
Look up, ye Briotns! ceafe to figh,
For your redemption draweth nigh.

See Penfion's harbour large and clear,
Defended by St. Stephen's pier!
The entrance fafe, by Current led,
Tiding round G—'s jetty head;
Look up, ye Britons! ceafe to figh,
For your redemption draweth nigh.

When

Of the profe compofitions of Chatterton,
his imitations of Offian are certainly the
worft: he has not indeed improved upon

an

When Civil-Power fhall fnore at eafe,
While foldiers fire—to keep the peace;
When murders fanctuary find,
And petticoats can Juftice blind;
Look up, ye Britons! ceafe to figh,
For your redemption draweth nigh.

Commerce o'er Bondage will prevail,
Free as the wind, that fills her fail.
When fhe complains of vile reftraint,
And Power is deaf to her complaint;
Look up, ye Britons! ceafe to figh,
For your redemption draweth nigh.

When raw projectors fhall begin
Oppreffion's hedge, to keep her in;
She in difdain will take her flight,
And bid the Gotham fools good night;
Look up, ye Britons! ceafe to figh,
For your redemption draweth nigh.

When tax is laid, to fave debate,
By prudent minifters of ftate;
And, what the people did not give,
Is levied by prerogative;
Look up, ye Britons! ceafe to figh,
For your redemption draweth nigh.

When Popifh bifhops dare to claim
Authority, in George's name;

By

an indifferent model. They are full of
wild imagery and inconfiftent metaphor,

with

By Treafon's hand fet up, in fpite
Of George's title, William's right;
Look up, ye Britons! ceafe to figh,
For your redemption draweth nigh.

When Popifh prieft a penfion draws
From ftarv'd exchequer, for the caufe
Commiffion'd, profelytes to make
In Britifh realms, for Britain's fake;
Look up, ye Britons! ceafe to figh,
For your redemption draweth nigh.

When fnug in power, fly recufants
Make laws for Britifh Proteftants;
And d——g William's Revolution,
As Juftices claim execution;
Look up, ye Britons! ceafe to figh,
For your redemption draweth nigh.

When foldiers, paid for our defence,
In wanton pride flay innocence;
Blood from the ground for vengeance reeks,
Till Heaven the inquifition makes;
Look up, ye Britons! ceafe to figh,
For your redemption draweth nigh.

When at Bute's feet poor Freedom lies,
Mark'd by the prieft for facrifice,
And doom'd a victim, for the fins
Of half the *outs*, and all the *ins*;
Look up, ye Britons! ceafe to figh,
For your redemption draweth nigh.

When

with little either of plot or of character
to recommend them.

His lighter Essays, such as the adventures of a star, the memoirs of a sad dog,

the

> When Stewards pass a *boot* account,
> And credit for the gross amount;
> Then to replace exhausted store,
> Mortgage the land to borrow more;
> Look up, ye Britons! cease to sigh,
> For your redemption draweth nigh.
>
> When scrutineers, for private ends,
> Against the vote declare their friends;
> Or judge, as you stand there alive,
> That five is more than forty-five;
> Look up, ye Britons! cease to sigh,
> For your redemption draweth nigh.
>
> When George shall condescend to hear
> The modest suit, the humble prayer;
> A prince, to purpled pride unknown!
> No favourites disgrace the throne!
> Look up, ye Britons! sigh no more,
> For your redemption's at the door.
>
> When time shall bring your wish about,
> Or, seven-years lease, *you sold*, is out;
> No future contract to fulfil;
> Your tenants holding at your will;
> Raise up your heads! your right demand!
> For your redemption's in your hand.

Then

the hunter of oddities, &c. difplay confiderable knowledge of what is called the
town, and demonftrate the keennefs of his
obfervation, and his quicknefs in acquiring any branch of knowledge, or in adapt-
ing himfelf to any fituation.   We are to
remember, however, that he had been long
converfant in this fpecies of compofition,
and that a confiderable fund of reading in
magazines, reviews, &c. which Mr. Warton obferves " form the *fchool of the people*," had prepared him well to exercife
the profeffion of a periodical writer.   Antiquities, however, conftituted his favorite ftudy, and in them his genius always
appears to the greateft advantage; even the
moft humorous of his pieces (Tony Sel-
wood's

Then is your time to ftrike the blow,
And let the *flaves* of Mammon know,
Britain's true fons A BRIBE can fcorn,.
And die as *free* as they were born.
VIRTUE again fhall take her feat,
And your redemption ftand compleat.

wood's letter *) derives its principal excellence from his knowledge of ancient
cuftoms.

In the volume of Mifcellanies attributed to him, there are fome pieces to which
his title is not well afcertained. Some
with the fignature of Afaphides, are claimed by one Lockftone, a linen-draper, and
a particular acquaintance of Chatterton;
and the ftory of Maria Friendlefs, which
Chatterton himfelf fent to the Town and
Country Magazine, probably for the fake
of obtaining an immediate and neceffary
fupply of money, is almoft a - literal
tranfcript of the letter of Mifella in the
Rambler.

If the reputation of Chatterton, however, refted folely on thofe works, which
he acknowledged as his own, it would
neither be fo extenfive as it is, nor probably

bably fo permanent as it is likely to continue. Rowley s poems have defervedly
immortalized the name of Chatterton,
and the controverfy which their publication excited, is the moft curious and extraordinary controverfy, which, fince the
days of Bentley has divided the literary
world.

I have already noticed the manner in
which thefe poems are faid to have been
difcovered. The account which Chatterton himfelf gave of the fuppofed author is nearly as follows:

THOMAS ROWLEY was born at Nor-
ton Mal-feward in Somerfetfhire, and
educated at the convent of St. Kenna, at
Keynefham * He was of the clerical
profeffion, was confeffor to the two
Canynge's, Robert and William, about the
latter end of the reign of Henry the VIth,

or

---

* Note prefixed to " Ballade of Charitie." Rowley's
poems, p. 203.

or about the beginning of that of Edward IV.; and was at leaft connected with
our lady's church in Briftol *; though he
is elfewhere ftyled the " parifh prieft of
St. John's, in the city of Briftol †." After
the death of Mr. Robert Canynge, (who
at his brother s defire, bequeathed Rowley 100 marks) he was employed by that
brother, Mr. William, to travel through
a confiderable part of England to collect
drawings. Mr. Canynge was fo well fatisfied with his fuccefs, that he rewarded
him with a purfe of two hundred pounds,
and promifed him that he fhould never
be in want. He continued afterwards
the confidential friend of Canynge. He
wrote a variety of poems, many of them
addreffed to that extraordinary character.
He firft lived in a houfe on the hill, and
afterwards

* Memoirs of Sir W. Canynge, Chatterton's Mifcellanies, p. 122.
† Introduction to the Battle of Haftings, Rowley's poems,
p. 21.

afterwards in one by the Tower *; he survived his patron, and died at Weftbury, in Glouceftershire †. Such is Chatterton's account; but it is only fair to mention, that the exiftence of any such person as Rowley, is totally denied by the difputants on one fide of the controverfy.

There can, however, be no doubt concerning the exiftence of W. Canynge, the patron of Rowley, fince it is attefted by fuch a number of contemporary hiftorians, and his remains lie interred in the church of which he was the founder. He is called by Chatterton, Sir William Canynge. He was the younger fon of a citizen of Briftol, and in his youth afforded early prognoftics of wifdom and ability. He was of a handfome perfon, and married for love, without a fortune. Soon after his marriage, his father and

L   his

* Chatterton's Mifcellanies, p. 127 & 128.
† Rowley's Poems, p. 203.

his eldeſt brother (who both loved money as much as he deſpiſed it) died, and left him large eſtates in land and money, and his brother John dependent upon him, whom he placed in ſuch an advantageous line of buſineſs, that he afterwards became Lord-Mayor of London.

This dawn of proſperity was, however, ſoon clouded by the death of his wife; to whoſe memory he afforded the moſt affectionate teſtimony, in rejecting the moſt ſplendid propoſals for a ſecond marriage. Of his native city he was Mayor five times; and in the year 1461, when Sir Baldwin Fulford was executed for treaſon, Canynge being then Mayor, pleaded for the criminal in vain. When he was knighted does not appear; but in the year 1467, a ſecond marriage being propoſed by the King, between him and one of the Widdeville, (the Queen's) family, Sir William went into holy orders purpoſely purpofely to avoid it; and was ordained Acolythe by his friend Carpenter, Bifhop of Worcefter, the 19th of September. He was afterwards dean of the Collegiate church of Weftbury in Wilts; with his ufual munificence he rebuilt that college, and died in the year 1474, with the univer- fal character of learning and virtue. Among the proofs of his munificence there ftill ex- ift an alms-houfe or hofpital, with a cha- pel, and the beautiful church of St. Mary Redcliffe, in Briftol *. At a great ex- penfe he had collected a cabinet of curi- ofities †; his collection of manufcripts, among which were copies of his own and Rowley's poems, were depofited in a room in Redcliffe church: of the actual or pretended difcovery of which I have already treated. Such is Chatterton's hiftory of Canynge, in which, though

L 2   there

Story of W. Canynge, Rowley's poems, Chatterton's Mifcellanies, p. 112 to 122.   † Ibid.

there are fome facts, which are amply
confirmed, there are alfo feveral which
are difputed by thofe who deny the authenticity of Rowley s poems.

Thefe poems, we have already feen,
were produced by Chatterton at different
times, who afferted that he had copied
them from the fragments of thofe ancient
parchments, which his father had procured from the Redcliffe cheft; he could
never be prevailed upon to produce any
originals, except a few fragments, the
largeft not more than eight inches long,
and four and a half wide. The writing
on thefe fragments was at leaft a tolerable imitation of ancient manufcript, and
the parchment or vellum had every mark
of age. The only poetical originals which
he produced were, the challenge to Lydgate, the fong to Ella, and Lydgate's anfwer, all contained in one parchment; the
account of W. Canynge's feaft; the epitaph

taph on Robert Canynge, and part of the
ftory of W. Canynge; befides thefe there
are fome profe compofitions, and a few
drawings, ftill in the hands of Mr. Barrett *.

The poems attributed to Rowley were
firft collected in an octavo volume, and
publifhed by Mr. Tyrwhitt, the learned
editor of Chaucer; a very fplendid edition was afterwards publifhed in quarto,
by the late Dr. Milles, dean of Exeter,
and prefident of the Society of Antiqua-
ries, with a preliminary differtation, and
notes tending to prove that they were
really written by Rowley and others in
the 15th century.

The

---

* A complete lift of the original parchments, which
were given to Mr. Barret by Chatterton, and which he has
now in his hands, was communicated by that gentleman to
Dr. Milles, and is as follows:

The Song to Ella, with the challenge to Lydgate and the
    Anfwer.

The poetical merit of thefe pieces is confiderable. The fubjects are interefting and infinite imagination is difplayed in the conftruction of the plots or fables, in the

arrangement

Anfwer. This poem was fent by Mr. Barret to a friend, and is unfortunately loft.

Canynge's Feaft, a Poem.

The firft thirty-fix lines of the Storie of William Canynge.

The following are Hiftorical Profe Compofitions.

1. The Yellow Roll, containing an account of the origin of coinage in England, and of the curiofities in Canynge's cabinet. This alfo was lent with the fong to Ella, by Mr. Barret to a friend, and is loft.

2. The purple Roll, thirteen inches by ten, containing an account of particular Coins, and the fecond and third Sections of Turgotus's Hiftory of Briftol. N. B. The firft Section above quoted is alfo extant in Chatterton's own hand, but the original does not appear.

3. Vita Burtoni, a parchment roll, about eight inches long, and four broad, very clofely written ; containing an account of Sir Simon de Burton, and his rebuilding Redclift church.

4. Knights Templars Church ; a Hiftory of its foundation, &c.

5. St. Mary's Church of the Port ; a Hiftory of it from its foundation, ending with the verfes on Robert Canynge.

6. Roll of Bartholomew's Priory, with a Lift of the Priors.

7. An

arrangement of the incidents, and the delineation of the characters. The beauties of poetry are scattered through them with no sparing hand. The Lyric productions in particular, such as the chorus's in the Tragedies, abound with luxuriant description, most vivid imagery, and striking metaphors. Through the veil of ancient language a happy adaptation of words

7. An account of the Chapel and House of Calendaries; a drawing of the chapel, and underneath an explanation of it.

8. Ella's Chapple.   No drawing, except to the Kist of Ella, but there is an account of its foundation.

9. St. Mary Magdalen's Chapel.   A drawing only.

10. Grey Friars Church.   A drawing only.

11. Drawing of three monumental Inscriptions.

12. Ancient Monument and Rudhall : mere delineations.

13. Lesser and Greater St. John's : only a rude delineation.

14. Several Drawings of the Castle of Bristol.

15. Strong Hold of the Castle : a drawing and account of its foundation, by Robert Earl of Gloucester, and Site thereof.

16. Old Wall of Bristol ; mere drawings.

17. Carne of Robert Curthose's Mynde in Castle steed : a drawing or figure, with the words *Carne*, &c. underneath.   Milles's Rowley, page 438.

words is ftill apparent, and a ftyle both
energetic and expreffive.   Contrary to almoft all the poetical productions of the
times, when they are fuppofed to have
been compofed, they are in general confpicuous for the harmony and elegance of
the verfe.   Indeed, fome paffages are inferior in none of the effentials of poetry,
to the moft finifhed productions of modern times.

On the other hand, it muft not be dif-
fembled that fome (and many will think
no inconfiderable) part of the charm of
thefe poems may probably refult from the
Gothic fublimity of the ftyle.   Whatever is vulgar in language is loft by time,
and a fmall degree of obfcurity in an ancient author gives a latitude to the fancy
of the reader, who generally imagines
the ftyle to be more forcible and expreffive than perhaps it intrinfically is.
We gaze with wonder on an antique fa-
brick,

brick; and when novelty of thought is not to be obtained, the novelty of language to which we are unaccuſtomed, is frequently accepted as a ſubſtitute. Moſt poets therefore, at leaſt ſuch as have aſpired to the ſublime, have thrown their dialect at leaſt a century behind the common proſe, and colloquial phraſelogy of their time; nor can we entertain a doubt but that even Shakeſpear and Milton have derived advantages from the antique ſtructure of ſome of their moſt admired paſſages. The facility of compoſition is alſo greatly increaſed where full latitude is permitted in the uſe of an obſolete dialect; ſince an author is indulged in the occaſional uſe of both the old and the modern phraſeology, and if the one does not ſupply him with the word for which he has immediate occaſion, the other in all probability will not diſappoint him.

That

That the subjects of Rowley's poems
are in general interesting and well chosen,
cannot, I think, be doubted by the judi-
cious reader, but still it must be confessed,
that the detail is occasionally heavy, flat,
and insipid. The imagery and metaphors
are frequently very common-place, and
it is possible to labour through several
stanzas without finding any striking beauty, when the attention of the reader is
kept alive by the subject alone. Many
defects of style, and many passages of rant
and bombast are concealed or excused by
the appearance of antiquity; and where
the harmony of the verse (which indeed
is not often the case) is, perhaps, radically
deficient, we are inclined to attribute it to
a different mode of accenting, or to our ignorance of the ancient pronunciation.

The piece of most conspicuous merit
in the collection is Ella, a Tragical In-
terlude, which is a most complete and
well-

well-written tragedy.   The plot is both
interefting and full of variety, though the
dialogue is in fome places tedious.   The
character of Celmonde reminds us of
Glenalvon in Douglas, but it is better
drawn : His foliloquy is beautiful and
characteriftic *.   The firft chorus, or
" Mynftrelles Songe" in this piece, is a
perfect

* C E L M O N D E.

Hope, hallie fufter, fweepeynge thro' the fkie,
In crowne of gouldé, and robe of lillie whyte,
Whyche farre abrode ynne gentle ayre doe flie,
Meetynge from diftaunce the enjoyous fyghte,
Albeytte efte thou takeft thie hie flyghte
Hecket ¹ ynne a myfte, and wyth thyne eyne yblente,
Nowe commeft thou to mee wythe ftarrie lyghte ;
Ontoe thie vefte the rodde fonne ys adente ² ;
The Sommer tyde, the month of Maie appere,
Depyéte wythe fkylledd honde upponn thie wyde aumere.

I from a nete of hopelen am adawed,
Awhaped ³ atte the fetyvenefs of daie ;
Ælla, bie nete moe thann hys myndbruche awed,
Is gone, and I mofte followe, toe the fraie.
Celmonde canne ne'er from anie byker ftaie.
Dothe warre begynne ? there's Clemonde yn the place.

Botte

¹ Wrapped clofely, covered.   ² faftened.   ³ aftonifh'd.

perfeɛt paſtoral. It abounds in natural
and tender ſentiments, and appoſite imagery, and the fertility of the author's gè-
nius

Botte whanne the warre ys donne, I'll haſte awaie.
The reſte from nethe tymes maſque muſt ſhew yttes face.
I ſee onnombered joies arounde mee ryſe ;
Blake ¹ ſtondethe future doome, and joie dothé mee alyſe.

O honnoure, honnoure, whatt ys bie thee hanne ?
Hailie the robber and the bordelyer,
Who kens ne thee, or ys to thee beſtanne,
And nothynge does thie myckle gaſtneſs fere.
Faygne woulde I from mie boſomme alle thee tare.
Thou there dyſperpelleſt ² thie levynne-bronde ;
Whyleſt mie ſoulgh's forwyned, thou art the gare;
Sleene ys mie comforte bie thie ſerie honde ;
As ſomme talle hylle, whann wynds doe ſhake the ground,
Itte kerveth all abroade, bie braſteynge hyltren wounde.

Honnoure, whatt bee ytte ? tys a ſhadowes ſhade,
A thynge of wychencref, an idle dreme ;
On of the ſonnis whych the clerche have made
Menne wydhoute ſprytes, and wommen for to ſleme ;
Knyghtes, who efte kenne the loude dynne of the beme,
Schulde be forgarde to ſyke enfeeblynge waies,
Make everych aɛte, alyche theyr ſoules, be breme,
And for theyre chyvalrie alleyne have prayſe.
    O thou, whatteer thie name,
      Or Zabalus or Queed,
    Comme, ſteel mie ſable ſpryte,
      For fremde 3 and dolefulle dede.

      ı Naked,   2 Scattereſt,   3 Strange.

nius is difplayed in this little ballad; fince fhort as it is, it contains a complete plot or fable *.

There

MANNE.

Tourne thee to thie Shepfterr ¹ fwayne;
Bryghte fonne has ne droncke the dewe
From the floures of yellowe hue;
Tourne thee, Alyce, backe agayne.

WOMANNE.

No, beftoikerre ², I wylle go,
Softlie tryppynge o'ere the mees 3,
Lyche the fylver-footed doe,
Seekynge fhelterr yn grene trees.

MANNE.

See the mofs-growne daifey'd banke,
Pereynge ynne the ftreme belowe;
Here we'lle fytte, yn dewie danke;
Tourne thee, Alyce, do notte goe.

WOMANNE.

I've hearde erfte mie grandame faie,
Yonge damoyfelles fchulde ne bee,
Inne the fwotie moonthe of Maie,
Wythe yonge menne bie the grene wode tree.

MANNE.

Sytte thee, Alyce, fytte and harke,
Howe the ouzle 4 chauntes hys noate,
The chelandree 5, greie morn larke,
Chauntynge from theyre lyttel throate;

WO-

1 Shepherd. 2 deceiver. 3 meadows. 4 The black-bird.
5 Goldfinch.

There are extant two parts or rather two different copies of the Battle of Haftings. Thefe

W O M A N N E.

I heare them from eche grene wode tree,
Chauntynge owte fo blataumtlie [1],
Tellynge lecturnyes [2] to mee,
Myfcheefe ys whanne you are nygh.

M A N N E.

See alonge the mees fo grene
Pied daifies, kynge-coppes fwote;
Alle wee fee, bie non bee feene,
Nete botte fhepe fettes here a fote.

W O M A N N E.

Shepfter fwayne, you tare mie gratche [3].
Oute uponne ye! lette me goe.
Leave mee fwythe, or I'lle alatche.
Robynne, thys youre dame fhall knowe.

M A N N E.

See! the crokynge brionie
Rounde the popler twyfte hys fpraie;
Rounde the oake the greene ivie
Florryfchethe and lyveth aie.

Lette us feate us bie thys tree,
Laughe, and fynge to lovynge ayres;
Comme, and doe notte coyen bee;
Nature made all thynges bie payres,

Drooried

1 Loudly.　2 lectures.　3 apparel.

These appear to have been higher in the estimation of Chatterton, as well as of Dr. Milles, than moft of the other productions

> Drooried cattes wylle after kynde;
> Gentle doves wylle kyfs and coe:
>
> #### WOMANNE.
>
> Botte manne, hee mofte bee ywrynde,
> Tylle fyr preefte make on of two.
>
> Tempe mee ne to the foule thynge;
> I wylle no mannes lemanne be;
> Tyll fyr preefte hys fonge doethe fynge,
> Thou fhalt neere fynde aught of mee.
>
> #### MANNE.
>
> Bie oure ladie her yborne,
> To-morrowe, foone-as ytte ys daie,
> I'lle make thee wyfe, ne bee forfworne,
> So tyde me lyfe or dethe for aie.
>
> #### WOMANNE.
>
> Whatt dothe lette, botte thatte nowe
> Wee attenes [1], thos honde yn honde,
> Unto diviniftre [2] goe,
> And bee lyncked yn wedlocke bonde?
>
> #### MANNE.
>
> I agree, and thus I plyghte
> Honde, and harte, and all that's myne;
> Good fyr Rogerr, do us ryghte,
> Make us one, at Cothbertes fhryne.
>
> #### BOTHE.

---

[1] At once.   [2] a divine.

ductions of Rowley. When Chatterton brought the firſt part to Mr. Barret, being greatly preſſed to produce the poem in the original hand-writing, he at laſt ſaid, that he had written this poem himſelf for a friend; but that he had another, the copy of an original by Rowley: and being then deſired to produce that poem, he brought, after ſome time, to Mr. Barrett, the poem which is marked in Mr. Tyrwhit's and Dr. Milles's editions, as No. 2 *.

The firſt of theſe poems I cannot help claſſing among the moſt inferior of Rowley's. The mere detail of violence and carnage, with nothing to intereſt curioſity, or engage the more tender paſſions,

can

BOTHE.

We wylle ynn a bordelle ¹ lyve,
Hailie, thoughe of no eſtate;
Everyche clocke moe love ſhall gyve;
Wee ynn godeneſſe wylle bee greate.

¹ A cottage.

* Introl. Account prefixed to Rowley's poems, p. 21.

can be pleafing to few readers. There is not a fingle epifode to enliven the tedious narrative, and but few of the beauties of poetry to relieve the mind from the dif-gufting fubject.

The fecond part is far fuperior. There is more of poetical defcription in it, more of nature, more of character. The im-agery is more animated, the incidents more varied. The character of Tancar-ville is well drawn, and the fpirit of can-dour and humanity which pervades it, is perhaps unparalleled in any writer before the age of Shakefpear. The whole epi-fode of Gyrtha is well conducted, and the altercation between him and his brother Harold, is interefting. But the defcrip-tion of morning *, and that of Salifbury

plain

---

* And now the greie- eyd morne with vi'lets dreft,
  Shakyng the dewdrops on the flourie meedes,
  Fled with her rofie radiance to the Weft :
  Forth from the Eafterne gatte the fyerie fteedes

M   Of

plain *, would be alone fufficient to ref-
cue the whole poem from oblivion, and
to entitle it to a place upon a claffic fhelf.

The

Of the bright funne awaytynge fpirits leedes :
The funne, in fierie pompe enthrond on hie,
Swyfter than thoughte alonge hys jernie gledes,
And fcatters nyghtes remaynes from oute the fkie :
He fawe the armies make for bloudie fraie,
And ftopt his driving fteeds, and hid his lyghtfome raye.

* Where fruytlefs heathes and meadows cladde in greie,
Save where derne hawthornes reare theyr humble heade,
The hungrie traveller upon his waie
Sees a huge defarte alle arounde hym fpredde,
The diftaunte citie fcantlie to be fpedde,
The curlynge force of fmoke he fees in vayne,
Tis too far diftaunte, and hys onlie bedde
Iwimpled in hys cloke ys on the playne,
Whylfte rattlynge thonder forrey oer his hedde,
And raines come down to wette hys harde uncouthlie bedde.

A wondrous pyle of rugged mountaynes ftandes,
Placd on eche other in a dreare arraie,
It ne could be the worke of human handes,
It ne was reared up bie menne of claie.
Here did the Brutons adoration paye
To the falfe god whom they did Tauran name,
Dightynge hys altarre with greete fyres in Maie,
Roaftynge their vyctualle round aboute the flame,
'Twas here that Hengyft did the Brytons flee,
As they were mette in council for to bee.

The utmoſt efforts of the author, however, cannot always impart intereſt or variety to the dull catalogue of names, which have ceaſed to be rememberéd, and the unvaried recital of wounds and deaths.   But Homer himſelf nods when engaged upon a topic ſo unfavourable to genius.

The Briſtowe Tragedy, or the Deathe of Syr Charles Bawdin, has little but its pathetic ſimplicity to recommend it.   There is nothing ingenious in the plot, or ſtriking in the execution; and it only ranks upon a par with a number of tragic ballads, both ancient and modern, in the ſame ſtyle.

The eclogues are to be accounted ſome of the moſt perfect ſpecimens among the poems of Rowley.   Indeed, I am not acquainted with any paſtorals ſuperior to them, either ancient or modern.   The firſt of them bears a remote reſemblance to the firſt eclogue of Virgil;

and contains a beautiful and pathetic pic-
ture of the ftate of England, during the
civil wars between the houfes of York
and Lancafter. The thoughts and images are all truly paftoral; and it is impoffible to read it, without experiencing
thofe lively, yet melancholy feelings,
which a true delineation of nature alone
can infpire. I cannot help feeling an
irrefiftable inclination to prefent the reader with two ftanzas, which have ever
appeared to me particularly beautiful.

RAUFE.

Saie to mee nete; I kenne thie woe in myne;
O! I've a tale that Sabalus 1 mote 2 telle.
Swote 3 flouretts, mantled meedows, foreftes dygne 4;
Gravots 5 far-kend 6 arounde the Errmiets 7 cell;
The fwote ribible 8 dynning 9 yn the dell;
The joyous daunceynge ynn the hoaftrie 10 courte;
Eke 11 the highe fonge and everych joie farewell,
Farewell the verie fhade of fayre dyfporte 12:
Impeftering 13 trobble onn mie heade doe comme,
Ne on kynde Seynfte to warde 14 the aye 15 encreafyngedome.

R O-

---

1 The Devil.   2 might.   3 fweet.   4 good, neat, genteel:
5 groves, fometimes ufed for a coppice.   6 far-feen.   7 Hermit.
8 violin.   9 founding.   10 inn, or public-houfe.   11 alfo.   12 pleafure.   13 annoying.   14 to keep off.   15 ever, always.

ROBERTE.

Oh! I coulde waile mie kynge-coppe-decked mees 16,
Mie fpreedynge flockes of fhepe of lillie white,
Mie tendre applynges 17, and embodyde 18 trees,
Mie Parker's Grange 19, far fpreedynge to the fyghte,
Mie cuyen 20 kyne 21, mie bullockes ftringe 22 yn fyghte.
Mie gorne 23 emblaunched 24 with the comfreie 25 plante,
Mie floure 26 Seyncte Marie fhotteyng wyth the lyghte,
Mie ftore of all the bleffynges Heaven can grant.
I amm dureffed 27 unto forrowes blowe,
Ihanten'd 28 to the peyne, will lette ne falte teare flowe.

16 Meadows. 17 grafted trees. 18 thick, ftout. 19 liberty of paf-
ture given to the Parker. 20 tender. 21 cows. 22 ftrong. 23 gar-
den. 24 whitened. 25 cumfrey, a favourite difh at that time.
26 marygold. 27 hardened. 28 accuftomed.

The fecond eclogue is an eulogium on
the actions of Richard I. in the Holy-
land, which will be read with additional
pleafure by thofe who have feen the fhort
but fpirited fketch of thefe wars in Mr.
Gibbon's laft volumes. The poem is
fuppofed to be fung by a young fhepherd,
whofe father is abfent on the Holy war:
and the Epode, or burthen, is happily
imagined:

  " Sprytes of the bleft, and every feyncte ydedde,
  " Pour out your pleafaunce on my fadre's hedde.

B fore

Before he has concluded his fong, he is cheered by the fight of the veffel in which his father returns victorious.

The third paftoral is chiefly to be admired for its excellent morality; it is, however, enlivened by a variety of appropriate imagery, and many of the ornaments of true poetry.

The laft of thefe paftorals, called Elinoure and Juga, is one of the fineft pathetic tales I have ever read. The complaint of two young females lamenting their lovers flain in the wars of York and Lancafter, was one of the'happieft fubjects that could be chofen for a tragic paftoral. Two ftanzas of this poem, will, I flatter myfelf, amply juftify this opinion: part of the former has been fuppofed, by the Anti-Rowleians, to be an imitation of a ftanza in Mr. Gray's elegy,

" The breezy call of incenfe breathing morn, &c."

E L I N,

ELINOURE.

No moe the mifkynette ¹ fhall wake the morne,
The minftrelle daunce, good cheere, and morryce plaie;
No moe the amblynge palfrie and the horne
Shall from the leffel ² rouze the foxe awaie;
I'll feke the forefte alle the lyve-longe daie;
Alle nete amenge the gravde chyrche 3 glebe will goe,
And to the paffante Spryghtes lecture 4 mie tale of woe.

JUGA.

Whan mokie 5 cloudis do hange upon the leme
Of leden ⁶ Moon, ynn fylver mantels dyghte;
The tryppeynge Faeries weve the golden dreme
Of Selynefs 7, whyche flyethe wythe the nyghte;
Thenne (botte the Seynctes forbydde!) gif to a fpryte
Syrr Rychardes forme ys lyped, I'll holde dyftraughte
Hys bledeynge claie-colde corfe, and die eche daie ynn
thoughte.

1 A fmall bagpipe.   2 in a confined fenfe, a bufh or hedge, though
fometimes ufed as a foreft.   3 church-yard.   4 relate.   5 black,
6 decreafing.   7 happinefs.

The ballad of Charity is an imitation
of the moft beautiful and affecting of our
Saviour's parables, the good Samaritan.——
The poetical defcriptions are truly pic-
turefque. We feel the horror of the
dark, cold night; we fee "the big drops
fall," and the "full flocks driving o'er

M 4   the

the plain." " The welkin opens, and
the yellow light'ning flies." " The thun-
der's rattling found moves flowly on, and
fwelling, burfts into a violent crafh; fhakes
the high fpire," &c.   If Chatterton
were really the author of this poem, he
probably alluded to his own deferted fituation, fince, it is faid, he gave it to the
publifher of the Town and Country Magazine, only a month before his death:

" Hafte to thie church-glebe houfe 1 afhrewed 2 manne!
" Hafte to thie kifte 3, thie only dortoufe 4 bedde.
" Cale as the claie, whiche will gre on thie hedde,
" Is charitie and love aminge 5 highe elves;
" Knights and barons live for pleafure and themfelves."

1 The *grave*.   2 *unfortunate*.   3 *coffin*.   4 *a fleeping room*.   5 *among*

The leffer pieces in this collection are
not without merit.   There is much elegant fatire in the two epiftles to Canynge
prefixed to Ella * ; and fome ftrokes of
pleafantry in the " Storie of Canynge."

As

* I have felected the firft of thefe epiftles as a fpecimen
of the fatiric powers of Rowley   Tys

As a complete fpecimen of this author's abilities in Lyric compofition, it is only neceffary

Tys fonge bie mynftrelles, thatte yn auntyent tym,
Whan Reafonn hylt ¹ herfelfe in cloudes of nyghte,
    The preefte delyvered alle the lege 2 yn rhym ;
    Lyche peynĉted 3 tyltynge fpeares to pleafe the fyghte,
    The whyche yn yttes felle ufe doe make moke 4 dere 5,
Syke dyd theire auncyante lee deftlie 6 delyghte the eare.

Perchaunce yn Vyrtues gare 7 rhym mote bee thenne,
Butte efte 8 nowe flyeth to the odher fyde ;
    In hallie 9 preefte apperes the ribaudes ¹⁰ penne,
    Inne lithe ¹¹ moncke apperes the barronnes pryde ;
    But rhym wythe fomme, as nedere ¹² widhout teethe,
Make pleafaunce to the fenfe, botte maie do lyttel fcathe ¹³.

Syr Johne, a knyghte, who hath a barne of lore ¹⁴,
Kenns ¹⁵ Latyn att fyrft fyghte from Frenche or Greke,
    Pyghethe ¹⁶ hys knowlachynge ¹⁷ ten yeres or more,
    To rynge upon the Latynne worde to fpeke.
    Whoever fpekethe Englyfch ys defpyfed,
The Englyfch hym to pleafe mofte fyrfte be latynized.

Vevyan, a moncke, good a requiem ¹⁸ fynges ;
Can preache fo wele, eche hynde ¹⁹ hys meneynge knowes ;
    Albeytte thefe gode guyfts awaie he flynges,
    Beeynge as badde yn vearfe as goode yn profe.
    Hee fynges of feynĉtes who dyed for yer Godde,
Everych wynter nyghte afrefche he fheddes theyr blodde.

To

---

1 Hid, concealed. 2 law. 3 painted. 4 much. 5 hurt, damage. 6 fweetly. 7 caufe. 8 oft. 9 holy. 10 rake, lewd perfon. 11 humble. 12 adder. 13 hurt, damage. 14 learning. 15 knows. 16 plucks or tortures. 17 knowledge. 18 a fervice ufed over the dead. 19 peafan

necessary to cite the incomparable ode or
chorus

To maydens, huswyfes, and unlored 20 dames,
Hee redes hys tales of merryment & woe.
Loughe 21 loudie dynneth 22 from the dolte 23 adrames 24;
He swelles on laudes of fooles, tho' kennes 25 hem soe.
Sommetyme at tragedie theie laughe and synge,
A merrie yaped 26 fage 27 somme hard-drayned water brynge.

Yette Vevyan ys ne foole, beyinde 28 hys lynes.
Geofroie makes vearse, as handycrafts theyr ware;
Wordes wythoute sense fulle groffyngelye 29 he twynes,
Cotteynge hys storie off as wythe a sheere;
Waytes monthes on nothynge, & hys storie donne,
Ne moe you from ytte kenn, than gyf 30 you neere begonne.

Enowe of odhers; of mieselfe to write,
Requyrynge whatt I doe notte nowe possess,
To you I leave the taske; I kenne your myghte
Wyll make mie faultes, mie meynte 31 of faultes, be'less.
ÆLLA wythe thys I sende, and hope that you
Wylle from ytte caste awaie, whatte lynes maie be untrue.

Playes made from hallie 32 tales I holde unmeete;
Lette somme greate storie of a manne be songe;
Whanne, as a manne, we Godde and Jesus treate,
In mie pore mynde, we doe the Godhedde wronge.
Botte lette ne wordes, whyche 33 droorie mote ne heare,
Bee placed yn the same.   Adieu untyll anere 34.

                              THOMAS ROWLEIE.

20 Unlearned.   21 laugh.   22 sounds.   23 foolish.   24 churls.
25 knows.   26 laughable.   27 tale, jest.   28 beyond.   29 foolishly.
30 if.   31. many.   32 holy.   33 strange perversion of words.   *Droori*
in its ancient signification stood for *modesty*.   34 another.

chorus in Goddwyn, a tragedy, which he
has left imperfect.

CHORUS, &c.

When Freedome, drefte yn blodde-fteyned vefte,
  To everie knyghte her warre-fonge funge,
Uponne her hedde wylde wedes were fpredde;
  A gorie anlace bye her honge.
    She daunced onne the heathe;
    She hearde the voice of deathe;
Pale-eyned affryghte, hys harte of fylver hue,
In vayne affayled 1 her bofomme to acale 2 ;
She hearde onflemed 3 the fhriekinge voice of woe,
And fadneffe ynne the owlette fhake the dale.
    She fhooke the burled 4 fpeere,
    On hie fhe jefte 5 her fheelde,
    Her foemen 6 all appere,
    And flizze 7 alonge the feelde.
Power, wythe his heafod 8 ftraught 9 ynto the fkyes,
Hys fpeere a fonne-beame, and his fheelde a ftarre,
Alyche 10 twaie 11 brendeynge 12 gronfyres 13 rolls hys eyes,
Chaftes 14 with hys yronne feete and foundes to war.
    She fyttes upon a rocke,
    She bendes before hys fpeere,
    She ryfes from the fhocke,
    Wielding her owne in ayre.
Harde as the thonder dothe fhe drive ytte on,
Wytte fcillye 15 wympled 16 gies 17 ytte to his crowne,

                Hys

1 Endeavoured.   2 freeze.   3 undifmayed.   4 armed, pointed.
5 hoifted on high, raifed. 6 foes, enemies. 7 fly. 8 head. 9 ftretched.
10 like.   11 two.   12 flaming.   13 meteors.   14 beats, ftamps.
15 clofely.   16 mantled, covered.   17 guides.

Hys longe fharpe fpere, hys fpreddynge fheelde is gon,
He falles, and fallynge rolleth thoufandes down.
   War, goare.faced war, bie envie burld 18, arift 19,
Hys feerie heaulme 20 noddynge to the ayre,
Tenne bloddie arrowes ynne hys ftreynynge fyfte—

*   *   *   *   *   *   *   *

        18 Armed.   19 arofe.   20 helmet.

The poems of Rowley had not been
long made public before their authenticity underwent a fevere fcrutiny; and a
number of gentlemen converfant in antiquities, declared, that they could not be the
productions of the fifteenth century, and
openly pronounced them the forgeries of
Chatterton. Their authenticity was defended by other perfons of no inconfiderable note in the literary world. The controverfy foon became voluminous; and
the reader will not be inclined to confider
it as unimportant, when on one fide the
names of Walpole, Tyrwhitt, Warton*,
                         Croft,

   * I have been well informed that both Mr. Warton and
Mr. Tyrwhit were formerly of fentiments directly oppofite
to thofe which they profefs in their publications; if the
poems therefore be forgeries of Chatterton, thefe gentlemen
were at leaft among the firft on whom he impofed.

Croft, and Malone, are mentioned : and
on the other, thofe of Milles and Bryant ;
and I think I may venture to add, that
of Mr. Matthias, though his candour and
modefty, almoft exempt him from being
confidered as a partizan.

I fhall endeavour to exhibit a fhort
fketch of the arguments on both fides of
the queftion, and fhall leave my readers to
form their own conclufions.

The evidence on this fubject naturally divides itfelf into two branches, external and internal : of the former, there
is little fatisfactory to be obtained ; and it
muft be confeffed, that the bulk of the
external evidence is rather againft that
party which denies the authenticity of the
poems. There are, however, a few facts
on that fide of the queftion which are
of too much confequence to be difre-
garded.

ARGU-

ARGUMENTS AGAINST the AUTHEN-
TICITY of ROWLEY'S POEMS.

External Evidence.

I. The firſt ſerious objection which occurs againſt the authenticity of the poems,
is, that Chatterton never could be prevailed
upon to produce more than four of the
originals, and theſe extremely ſhort, the
whole not containing more than 124
verſes *.   Had ſuch a treaſure of ancient
poetry fallen into the hands of a young
and ingenuous perſon, would he, it is ſaid,
have cautiouſly produced them to the
world one by one ?   Would he not rather
have been proud of his good fortune ?
Would not the communicativeneſs of youth
have induced him to blaze the diſcovery
abroad, and to call every lover of poetry
and antiquity, to a participation of the
pleaſure ?

* Tyrwhitt's Vindication, p. 133.

pleafure ? Would not the hope and offers of reward at leaft have prevented his deftroying what, if preferved, would certainly be productive of profit, but the deftruction of which could anfwer no purpofe whatever * ?

II. The deficiency of proof in favour of Rowley, is ftrongly aided by the very probable proofs in favour of Chatterton. His abilities were in every refpect calculated for fuch a deception. He had been in the habit of writing verfes from his earlieft youth, and produced fome excellent poetry. He was known to have been converfant with our old Englifh poets and hiftorians, particularly Chaucer. His fondnefs for heraldry, introduced many books of antiquities to his notice; and

even

---

* An examination, &c. p. 9. Tyrwhitt's Vindication, p. 155. See alfo fome excellent remarks to the fame purpofe, by the late Mr. Badcock, Monthly Review for May, 1782.

even his profeffion difpofed him to thefo
ftudies, and enabled him with facility to
imitate ancient writings. In *the Chriftmas
games;* which are acknowledged to be his
own, there is much of that peculiar
learning in Britifh antiquities, which was
neceffary to lay the foundation of Rowley's poems; and in his Effay on Sculp-
ture, there is much of the fame general
information with which thofe compofitions abound * The tranfport and delight,

* In the fupplement to the works of Chatterton, (printed
for Becket, 1784,) there is inferted a piece which has
been already referred to, called Chatterton's will. This
appears to have been written a few days before he left
Briftol to go to London ; when in confequence, as it fhould
feem, of his being refufed a fmall fum of money by a
gentleman, whom he had occafionally complimented in his
poems, he had taken a refolution of deftroying himfelf the
next day. What prevented him from carrying this defign
at that time into execution does not appear ; but the
whole writing on this occafion is worth attention, as it
throws much light on his real charaƈer, his acquaintance
with old Englifh writers, and his capability of underftanding and imitating old French and Latin infcriptions, not
indeed gramatically, but fufficient to anfwer the purpofes
to

light which Chatterton always difcovered
on reading the poems to Mr. Smith, his
fifter, and his different friends, could not,
it is faid, have refulted from the mere
pleafure of a difcovery : it was the fecret, but ardent feeling of his own abilities, and the confcioufnefs that the praifes
which were beftowed upon them were all
his own, which filled him with exultation,

and

to which he often applied this knowledge. From this
writing it alfo appears that he would not allow King David
to have been a holy man, from the ftrains of piety and
devotion in his pfalms, becaufe a *great genius can effect any
thing* ; that is, *affume* any *character* and *mode* of *writing* he
pleafes. This is an anfwer from Chatterton himfelf, to one
argument, and a very powerful one, in fupport of the authenticity of Rowley's poems. In that part of the will addreffed to Mr. George Catcot, Chatterton mentions Rowley's poems, but in fo guarded a manner, that it is not
eafy to draw any certain information for or againft their
authenticity ; though the parties on both. fides have attempted it.   The addrefs to Mr. Barrett does no lefs
credit to his own feelings, than to that gentleman's treatment of him ; and the apology that follows to the two Mr.
Catcotts, for fome effufions of his fatire upon them, is
the beft recompence he then had in his power to make to
thofe gentlemen, from whom he had experienced much
civility and kindnefs. O.

N

and produced thofe ftrong emotions, which even his habitual referve on this fubject was unable to conceal *.

III. The declaration of Chatterton to Mr. Barrett, concerning the firft part of the Battle of Haftings, which he con-feffed *he had written himfelf*, is a pre-fumption againft the reft. He was then taken by furprize, but at other times preferved a degree of confiftency in his falfehood.

IV. Mr. Ruddall, an intimate acquain-tance of Chatterton, declared to Mr. Croft, that he faw him (Chatterton) dif-guife feveral pieces of parchment with the appearances of age, and that Chatter-ton told him, that the parchment which Mr. Ruddall had affifted him in black-ing and difguifing, was the very parch-ment he had fent to the printer's, con-

taining

taining " the account of the Fryers paffing the old bridge *."

V. The

* " To George Steevens, Efq. Hampftead Heath.

" Dear Sir,

" IT gives me pleafure that Love and Madness, which
I put together in a few idle hours, as much for the fake of
doing juftice to poor Chatterton as of blunting the edge of
Hackman's fhocking example, has fo well anfwered the
former purpofe.

    " ————— Where'er (his bones at refte)
   " His fpryte to haunte delyghteth befte,"
Chatterton muft be now not a little gratified when he looks
down upon the fquabbles he has raifed on earth. Every
fyllable which I have made Hackman relate of him in Love
and Madness is, I firmly believe, religioufly true.
Walmfly was my tenant for the houfe in Shoreditch, where
Chatterton lodged with h m, at the time he gave me the
information contained in my book. Chatterton's letters
which I printed, and which are hardly lefs fingular perhaps
than Rowley's poems, are confeffedly original.

" As I cannot fpare time from my profeffion to enter any
further into this difpute, and as you inform me that Mr.
Warton is going to publifh fomething, I write this letter,
according to your defire, in anfwer to your's of yefterday,
refpecting what long fince I faid to you of Mr. Ruddall ;
and it is perfectly at Mr. Warton's fervice. But I muft
defire he will print it exactly as I fend it you. When I
have fpoken for myfelf, he may draw his own arguments
from my communication.

     " The

V. The Rev. Mr. Catcott, brother to the Mr. Catcott before mentioned, affirmed,

" The left hand column is an extract from Dean Milles's quarto edition of Rowley's, i. e. of Chatterton's poems, p. 436, 7. The right hand column is my account of the same bufinefs. In fome material circumftances he certainly errs. It were eafy to fhew, the Dean has condemned Chatterton, and robbed him of Rowley's poems upon flighter evidence of lefs material miftakes.

" That the Dean fhould have received *all* his information of this bufinefs from Mr. Ruddall, is certainly impoffible, becaufe fome part of his account of it is certainly untrue. The paffages in the Dean's account, on which I comment, are marked, that they may be printed in Italics.

" A *fingular* circumftance relating to the hiftory of this ceremony (" of paffing the " old bridge") *has been communicated to the Publick within thefe two laft years;* and candour requires that it fhould not pafs unnoticed here, efpecially as the character of the relator leaves no room for fufpicion. The objectors to the authenticity of thefe poems may poffibly triumph in the difcovery of a fact, which contains, in their opinion, a decifive proof that Chatterton

The circumftance is fingular, and I have always thought fo ; but it has never yet, I believe, been *communicated to the Publick*; though I certainly meant it fhould fome time or other.

It

firmed, that having had a converfation one
evening with Chatterton, he traced the
very

Chatterton was the author of
this paper, and (as they
would infer) of all the poetry
which he produced under
Rowley's name; but, *when
the circumftances are attentively examined*, the reader
will probably find, that even
this fact tends rather to efta-
blifh, than to invalidate, the
authenticity of the poems.

Mr. John Ruddall, a na-
tive and inhabitant of Briftol,
and formerly apprentice to
Mr. Francis Grefley, an apothecary in that city, was well
acquainted with Chatterton,
whilft he was apprentice to
Mr. Lambert. During that
time, Chatterton frequently
called upon him at his mafter's houfe, and, *foon after he
had printed this account of the
Bridge* in the Briftol paper,
*told Mr. Ruddall, that he
was the author of it; but, it
occuring to him afterwards,
that he might be called upon to
produce the original, he brought*
to

It is not clear to me, that
the advocates for Chatterton
have occafion to be apprehenfive, *if, the circumftances
fhould be attentively examined*
even according to the Dean's
own fhewing. But mine is
fomewhat different.

N 3

My

very fubftance of this cónverfation, in a piece which that indefatigable genius produced fometime after as Rowley's.

VI. Chat-

to him one day a piece of Parchment, about the fize of a half Sheet of Fool'sCap paper ; Mr. Ruddall does not think that any thing was written on it when produced by Chatterton, but he faw him write feveral Words, if not lines, in a Charaéter which Mr. Ruddall did not underftand, which he fays was totally unlike Englifh, and, as he apprehended, was meant by Chatterton, to imitate or reprefent the original from which this Account was printed. He cannot determine precifely how much Chatterton wrote in this manner, but fays, that the time he fpent in that Vifit did not exceed three quarters of an hour; the Size of the Parchment, however, (even fuppofing it to have been filled with writing) will in fome meafure afcertain the quantity which it contained,

My vifit to Briftol of a few days, in order to colleét information concerning Chatterton, was on the 23d of July, 1778. At that time I gave fomething to the Mother and Sifter for their voluntary communications to me. After I publifhed LOVE AND MADNESS, I laid a larger plan for their benefit, which I hope ftill to fee carried into execution ; and I deftined fomething more to the family of him whofe genius I fo much refpeéted, though I well knew his family deemed me their enemy for endeavouring to prove him guilty of Forgery. Prevented from going to Bath, and confequently from giving what I had fet apart for this purpofe, with my own Hands, I gladly feized the liberty allowed me by a friend of Mr. Ruddall to beg this favour of him, On

the

VI. Chatterton at firſt exhibited the Songe to Ella in his own hand-writing; and afterwards in the parchment, which he gave

the 22d of March, 1781, I wrote to Mr. Ruddall, to whom I was then a perfect ſtranger, making uſe of his Friend's name, and encloſing a Draught to him or his order for ten pounds, requeſting he would give the Money to Chatterton's Mother and Siſter. On the 30th of the ſame Month, Mr. Ruddall called upon me in Lincoln's Inn; appeared, as I imagined, to lean to the ſide of this queſtion which I have ever thought to be the right; and told me, of his own accord, what certainly agrees no more with the Dean's account, than what I have already related agrees with the Dean's ſaying that Mr. Ruddall told this, *in 1779, on the proſpect of procuring a gratuity of ten Pounds for Chatterton's Mother, from a Gentleman who came to Briſ-*

He   N 4   *tol*

gave to Mr. Barrett as the original, there were found feveral variations, which it is fuppofed

tol in order to collect informa-
tion concerning the Son's Hif-
tory.

He fays alfo, that *when Chatterton had written on the Parchment, he held it over the Candle, to give it the appearance of antiquity, which changed the Colour of the Ink, and made the Parchment appear black and a little contracted: he never faw him make any fimilar attempt, nor was the Parchment produced afterwards by Chatterton to him, or (as far as he knows) to any other perfon. From a perfect knowledge of Chatterton's abilities, he thinks him to have been incapable of writing the Battle of Haftings, or any of thofe Poems produced by him under the name of Rowley,* nor does he remember that Chatterton ever mentioned Rowley's Poems to him, either as original or the contrary; but fometimes (though very rarely) intimated

If my Memory not only fails me now, but failed me the fame day, and has failed me ever fince, Mr. Ruddall will correct me. To him I appeal, and by him I muft fubmit to be corrected. But, on the 30th of March, 1781, he told me, AS I THINK, that *he affifted Chatterton in difguifing* SEVERAL *pieces of Parchment with the appearances of Age, juft before " the " Account of paffing the " Bridge" appeared in Farley's Journal; that, after they had made feveral experiments, Chatterton faid, " this will " do, now I will black* THE *" Parchment;" that, whether he told him at the time what* THE *Parchment was, he could not remember; that he believed he did not fee Chatterton black* THE *Parchment, but that Chatterton told him,*

after

fupposed he had admitted through forget-
fulnefs, or perhaps, as actual corrections,
considering

mated that he was poffeffed of fome valuable literary productions. *Mr. Ruddall had promifed Chatterton not to reveal this Secret, and he fcrupuloufly kept his word till the year* 1779; *but,* ON THE PROSPECT OF PROCURING A GRATUITY OF TEN POUNDS, FOR CHATTERTON'S MOTHER, FROM A GENTLEMAN WHO CAME TO BRISTOL IN ORDER TO COLLECT INFORMATION CONCERNING HER SON'S HISTORY, he thought fo material a benefit to the Family would fully juftify him for divulging a fecret by which no perfon now living could be a fufferer."

after " *the Account of paf-* " *fing the Bridge*" *had appeared in the News-paper, that* THE *Parchment which he had blacked and difguifed, after their experiments, was what he had fent to the Printer containing the* ACCOUNT."

" As this appeared to me the moft decifive evidence, I afked Mr. Ruddall's leave to make ufe of his name about it, which he granted me; and I made a Memorandum of it, the fame day, at the diftance of a few hours. But it is ftill poffible my Memory might deceive me. In matters more ferious than the authenticity of Poems, which are certainly

considering that the parchment was the copy which probably would be reforted to as a ftandard *.

VII. The

certainly exquifite, whoever wrote them, it is not my way, I hope, to be more pofitive than I ought.

" Mr. Ruddall will excufe me if I fay, that I cannot pof-fibly allow him, or any one, to determine the authenticity of the Poems, by telling the Dean, or the world, that, " *from a perfect knowledge of Chatterton's abilities,* HE " thinks him to have been incapable of writing the Battle of " Haftings, or any of thofe Poems produced by him under " the name of Rowley."

" It appears to me that I cannot poffibly, all this time, have been noticing what does not relate to me, becaufe Chatterton's Sifter, when fhe thanks me in a Letter dated April the 20th, 1781, for what I fent her and her Mother, through Mr. Ruddall, fays, that " the only benefits they " have reaped from *the labours of her dear Brother,*" are what they have received from me.

" Convey this to Mr. Warton, if you choofe it, with many thanks for the pleafure I have received from his Hiftory of Englifh Poetry ; and believe me to be,

" Dear Sir,

" Your obliged friend,

Lincolns-inn,   " HERBERT CROFT, jun."
Feb. 5, 1782.

* Curfory Obfervations on Rowley's poems, p. 44.

VII. The hand-writing of the fragment containing the ftorie of W. Canynge, is quite different from the hand-
writing of that which contains " the
accounte of W. Canyinge's feaft;" and
neither of them is written in the ufual
record hand of the age to which they
are attributed. Indeed, in the " accounte
of W. Canynge's Feafte," the Arabian
numerals, (63) are faid to be perfectly
modern, totally different from the figures
ufed in the fifteenth century, and exactly
fuch as Chatterton himfelf was accuftomed to make *.

VIII. The very exiftence of any fuch
perfon as ROWLEY is queftioned, and upon apparently good ground. He is not fo
much as noticed by William of Worceftre,
who lived nearly about the fuppofed time
of Rowley, was himfelf of Briftol, and makes
frequent

* See Milles's Rowley, p. 429. Tyrwhitt's Vindication,
p. 135 Monthly Review, by Badcock, for March 1782.

frequent mention of Canynge. "Bale, who lived two hundred years nearer to Rowley than we, and who, by unwearried induſtry, dug a thouſand bad authors out of obſcurity," has never taken the leaſt notice of ſuch a perſon*; nor yet Leland, Pitts, or Tanner, nor indeed any other literary biographer. That no copies of any of his works ſhould exiſt, but thoſe depoſited in Redcliffe church, is alſo an unaccountable circumſtance not eaſy to be ſurmounted †.

IX. Objections are even made to the manner in which the poems are ſaid to have been preſerved. That title deeds relating to the church or even hiſtorical records might be lodged in the muniment room of Redcliffe church, is allowed to be ſufficiently probable; but that *poems* ſhould have been conſigned to a cheſt

* Walpole's two letters, p. 31. .
† Tyrwhitt's Vindication, p. 119, 121.

cheft with fix keys, kept in a private room in a church with title deeds and conveyances, and that thefe keys fhould be intrufted, not to the heads of a college, or any literary fociety, but to aldermen and church wardens, is a fuppofition replete with abfurdity; and the improbability is increafed, when we confider that thefe very papers paffed through the hands of perfons of fome literature, of Chatterton's father in particular, who had a tafte for poetry, and yet without the leaft difcovery of their intrinfic value *.

Internal Evidence.

I. In point of STYLE, COMPOSITION, nd SENTIMENT, it is urged by Mr. Warton, and thofe who adopt the fame fide of the controverfy, that the poems of Rowley are infinitely fuperior to every other production of the century, which is

faid

* See Monthly Review for March 1782.

said to have produced them. Our ancient poets are minute and particular,
they do not deal in abstraction and general
exhibition, but dwell on realities; but
the writer of these poems adopts ideal
terms and artificial modes of explaining
a fact, and employs too frequently the aid
of metaphor and personification *. Our
ancient bards abound in unnatural concep-
tions, strange imaginations, and even the
most ridiculous inconsistencies; but Rowley's poems present us with no incongru-
ous combinations, no mixture of manners, institutions, usages and characters:
they contain no violent or gross impro-
prieties †. One of the striking characteristics of old English poetry, is a continued tenor of disparity. In Gower,
Chaucer, and Lydgate, elegant descrip-
tions, ornamental images, &c. bear no
                            proportion

* Matthias's Essay on Evid, p. 64
† Warton's Inquiry, p. 21.

proportion to pages of languor, mediocrity, profaic and uninterefting details ; but the poems in queftion are uniformly fupported, and are throughout poetical and animated *. Poetry, like other fciences (fay thefe critics) has its gradual acceffions and advancements ; and the poems in queftion poffefs all that elegance, firmnefs of contexture, ftrength and brilliancy, which did not appear in our poetry before the middle of the prefent century.

II. There appears in thefe poems none of that LEARNING, which peculiarly marks all the compofitions of the fifteenth century. Our old poets are perpetually confounding Gothic and claffical allufions ; Ovid and St. Auftin are fometimes cited in the fame line. A ftudious ecclefiaftic of that period would give us a variety of ufelefs authorities
                                    from

* Ibid. p. 20; Monthly Review, May 1782,

from Ariftotle, from Boethius, and from
the Fathers : and the whole would be in-
terfperfed with allufions to another kind
of reading, viz. the old romances; the
round table, with Sir Launcelott, and
Sir Triftram, and Charlemagne, would
have been conftantly cited *. Poems from
fuch an author, would alfo have occafionally exhibited prolix devotional epifodes,
mingled with texts of Scripture, and ad-
dreffes to the Saints and bleffed Virgin;
inftead of apoftrophes to fuch allegori-
cal divinities as Truth and Content, and
others of Pagan original †.

As to the hiftorical allufions which are
really found in thefe poems, it is afferted,
that they are only fuch as might be fupplied by books which are eafily obtained,
fuch as Hollingfhead and Fox, Fuller's
church hiftory, Geofry of Monmouth, and
others

* Warton's Inquiry, 21, 97, 99.
† Ibid 98.

others of a fimilar nature *; and that general reading has been miftaken for profound erudition †.

II. Some ANACHRONISMS have alfo been pointed out in the manufcripts of Rowley. Thus the art of *knitting ftockings* is alluded to in the Tragedy of Ella ‡; whereas it is a well eftablifhed fact,

---

* Matthias's Effay, p. 69. An Examination of Rowley's Poems, p. 24.

† Warton's Inquiry.

‡ As Elynour bie the green leffelle was fyttynge,
    As from the fones hete fhe harried,
  She fayde, as herr whytte hondes whyte hofen was knyt tynge,
    Whattè pleafure ytt ys to be married!

Mie hufbande, Lorde Thomas, a forrefter boulde,
    As ever clove pynne, or the bafkette,
Does no cheryfauncys from Elynour houlde,
    I have ytte as foone as I afke ytte.

Whann I lyved wyth mie fadre yn merrie Clowd-dell,
    Tho' twas at my liefe to mynde fpynnynge,
I ftylle wanted fomethynge, botte whatte ne coulde telle,
    Mie lorde fadres barbde haulle han ne wynnynge.

O   Eche

fact, that the art was utterly unknown
in the reign of Edward IV. Briftol is
called a city, though it was not fuch till
long after the death of that monarch.
Canynge is faid to have poffeffed a *cabinet* of coins, *drawings*, &c. though thefe
words were not then in ufe; and *manufcripts* are fpoken of as rarities, at a time
when there were fcarcely any other books:
when, in truth, a printed book muft have
been a much greater curiofity *.

IV   The

Eche mónynge I ryfe, doe I fette mie maydennes,
    Somme to fpynn, fomme to curdell, fomme bleachynge,
Gyff any new entered doe afke for mie aidens,
    Thann fwythynne you fynde mee a teachynge.

Lorde Walterre, mie fadre, he loved me welle,
    And nothynge unto mee was nedeynge,
Botte fchulde I agen goe to merrie Cloud-dell,
    In fothen twoulde bee wythoute redeynge.

Shee fayde, and lorde Thomas came over the lea,
    As hee the fatte derkynnes wae chacynge,
Shee putte uppe her knyttynge, and to hym wente fhee;
    So wee leave hem bothe kyndelie embracynge.

* Curfcry Obfervations on Rowley's poems, p. 22—25.

IV. The METRE of the old Englifh poetry, is faid to be totally different from that of Rowley. The ftanza in which the majority of thefe poems are written, confifts of ten lines, the two firft qua-trains of which rhyme alternately, and it clofes with an alexandrine; no example of which occurs in Chaucer, Lydgate or Gower. Spencer extended the old octavo ftanza to nine lines, clofing with an alex-andrine, to which Prior added a tenth *. Above all, the extraordinary inftance of an Englifh Pindaric in the fifteenth century, is ridiculed by Mr. Warton, which no-velty (he fays) " was referved for the capricious ambition of Cowley's mufe." That Rowley fhould ever have feen the original model of this irregular ftyle of compofition, is utterly improbable, fince

O 2   Pindar

* Matthias's Effay, p. 66.

Pindar was one of the laſt claſſics that emerged at the reſtoration of literature *.

To this head may be refered the extraordinary *ſmoothneſs of the verſe,* which is utterly unparalleled in any poet for more than a century after the ſuppoſed age of Rowley †; the accent or cadence, which is always modern; and the perfection and harmony of the rhyme ‡.

V. While the compoſition, metre, &c. are wholly modern, the LANGUAGE is aſſerted to be too ancient for the date of the poems. It is not the language of any particular period, but of two entire centuries §. The diction and verſification are at perpetual variance ||. The author appears to have borrowed all his ancient language, not from the uſage of common life,

* Warton's Inquiry, p. 33, 39
† Curſory Obſervations, p. 5.
‡ Matthias's Eſſay, p. 67.
§ Curſory Obſervations, p. 32.
|| Warton's Inquiry, p. 42.

life, but from Speght, Skinner, and other lexicographers, and to have copied their miftakes *. He has even introduced words which never made a part of the Englifh language, and which are evidently the coinage of fancy, analogy, or miftake †.

VI. Notwithftanding this affectation of ancient language, it is added, that the tinfel of MODERN PHRASEOLOGY may in too many inftances be detected. Thus fuch phrafes as " *Puerilitie* ; *before* his *optics* ; *blamelefs* tongue; the aucthoure of the *piece*; veffel wreckt upon the *tragic* fand; the *proto-fleyne* man,"&c. could not be the language of the fifteenth century We find alfo a number of modern formularies and combinations, e. g. " Syfters in forrow ; poygnant arrowes *typp'd* with deftinie ; Oh, Goddes !

O 3　　　　Now

---

* Matthias's Effay, p. 68. Tyrwhitt's Appendix to Rowley's Poems, and Vindication paffim.
† Ibid.

Now by the Goddes ; Ah, what avaulde ;
Awaie, awaie ! (which is the cant of modern tragedy) Oh, thou, whate'er thie
name ;" with a number of compound epi-
thets *, and other almoſt certain marks
of modern compoſition †.

VIII. To theſe may be added ſome paſſages which appear to be imitations of
modern poets. Many of thoſe, which
have been cited to convict Chatterton of
plagiariſm, are, it muſt be confeſſed, ſuch
obvious thoughts, that they might be
adopted by a perſon who had never ſeen
the modern publications in which they
appear ; but ſuch coincidences as the following are palpable

> " O ! for a muſe of fire !"   Shakeſ. Hen. V.
> " O forre a ſpryte al feere !"   Ella, l. 729.
>
> " His beard all white as ſnow.
> " All flaxen was his pole."   Hamlet.

" Black

---

* Warton's Inquiry, p. 23, 24.
† Curſory Obſervations, p. 12, 13.

" Black his cryne as the winter nyghte,
" White his rode, as the fommer fnowe." Ella, l. 851,

" No, no, he is dead,
" Gone to his death bed."   Hamlet.

" Mie love is dedde,
" Gone to his deathe-bedde."   Ella, l. 855.

" Unhoufell'd, unanointed, *unaknell'd*,"
                                Hamlet in Pope's edit.
" Unburled, undelievre, unefpryte." Goddwyn, l. 27.
" Their fouls from corpfes *unaknell'd* depart."
                            Bat. of Haft. part 1, l. 288.

" The grey-goofe wing that was thereon,
" In his hearts-blood was wet."   Chevy Chace.

" The *grey-goofe* pynion, that *thereon* was fett,
" Eftfoons wyth fmokyng *crimfon bloud was wett*."
                            Bat. of Haft. part 1, l. 200.

With fuch a force and vehement might
   He did his body gore,
The fpear went thro' the other fide
   A large *cloth-yard* and *more.*   Chevy-Chace.

With thilk a force it *did his body gore,*
That in his tender guts it entered,
In veritie, a full *cloth-yard or more.*   Bat. of Haft *.

" Clos'd his eyes in endlefs night."   Gray's bard.
" He clos'd his eyne in everlaftynge nyghte."
                            Bat. of Haft. part 2. l. 278 †.
                    O 4   The

---
* See Monthly Review.
† See a letter prefixed to Chatterton's Mifcellanies, p. 24.

The advocates of Rowley, are, however, not deftitute of arguments in their fupport; I fhall therefore divide the evidence in the fame manner as in ftating the former, and endeavour to exhibit as fair a fummary as poffible.

ARGUMENTS TO PROVE THAT THE POEMS ATTRIBUTED TO ROWLEY, WERE REALLY WRITTEN BY HIM AND OTHERS IN THE 15th CENTURY.

External Evidence.

I. The firft grand argument which the advocates on this fide advance, is the conftant and uniform affertion (except in a fingle inftance) of Chatterton himfelf, who is reprefented by his fifter, and all his intimates, as a lover of truth from the earlieft dawn of reafon. He was alfo moft infatiable of fame, and abounded in vanity. He felt himfelf neglected, and many paf-

sages

fages of his writings are full of invective
on this fubject. Is it probable, that fuch
a perfon fhould barter the fair character of
truth, which he loved, for the fake of
perfifting in falfehood, which he detefted? Is it probable, that a perfon of his
confummate vanity, fhould uniformly give
the honour of all his more excellent compofitions to another, and only infcribe his
name to thofe which were evidently inferior? But even though a man might
be thus carelefs of his reputation during
his life time, under the conviction that
he might affume the honour whenever he
pleafed, would this carelefsnefs continue
even at the hour of death? Would he at
a moment, when he actually meditated
his own deftruction; in a paper which he
infcribes—" All this wrote between 11
and 2 o'clock Saturday (Evening), in the
utmoft diftrefs of mind,"—ftill repeat
with the utmoft folemnity the fame falfe
                                    affertion

affertion that he had affirmed during the former part of his life ? there was at leaft *no occafion* to introduce the fubject at that time, and he might have been filent, if he did not chufe to clofe his exiftence with a direct falfehood *. If we confider the joy which he manifefted on the difcovery of the parchments, the avidity with which he read them, he muft be the moft complete of diffemblers, if really they contained no fuch treafure as he pretended. To another very extraordinary circumftance Mr. Catcott has pledged himfelf, which is, that on his firft acquaintance with Chatterton, the latter mentioned by *name* almoft all the poems which have fince appeared in print, and that at a time, when, if he were the author, one-tenth of them could not be written †.

II. Next

---

* See Chatterton's will, Appendix to Mifcellanies. See alfo the learned Mr. Bryant's Obfervations, p. 499, 547,
† Ibid. 548.

II. Next to the affeverations of Chatterton himfelf, we are bound to pay at leaft fome attention to thofe of all his friends. His mother accurately remembers the whole tranfaction concerning the parchments, as I have already ftated it. His fifter alfo recollects to have feen the original parchment of the poem on our Lady's Church, and, fhe thinks, of the Battle of Haftings: fhe remembers to have heard her brother mention frequently the names of Turgot, and of John Stowe, befides that of Rowley. * Mr. Smith, who was one of the moft intimate friends of Chatterton, remembers to have feen manufcripts upon vellum, to the number of a dozen in his poffeffion, many of them ornamented with the heads of kings or of popes, and fome of them as broad as the bottom of a large fized chair †. He

ufed

---

* Milles's Preliminary Differtation, p. 8.
† Bryant's Obfervations, p. 528.

ufed frequently to read to Mr. Smith, fometimes parts, and fometimes whole treatifes from thefe old manufcripts; and Mr. Smith has very often been prefent while he tranfcribed them at Mr. Lambert's *. Mr. Capel, a jeweller, at Briftol, affured Mr. Bryant, that he had frequently called upon Chatterton, while at Mr. Lambert's, and had at times found him tranfcribing ancient manufcripts anfwering to the former defcription †. Mr. Thiftlethwaite, in the curious letter already quoted, relates, that during the year 1768, " at divers vifits, he found Chatterton employed in copying Rowley from what he ftill confiders as undoubted originals ‡." Mr. Carey alfo, another intimate acquaintance, frequently heard Chatterton mention thefe manufcripts foon after he left Colfton's fchool. Every

one

* Bryant's Obfervations.
† Ibid, p. 523.
‡ Milles's Rowley, p. 457.

one of thefe gentlemen, as well as Mr. Clayfield and Mr. Ruddall, declare unequivocally, from an intimate knowledge of Chatterton's learning and abililies, that they believe him incapable of producing the poems of Rowley.

III. That a number of manufcripts were found in Redcliffe church, cannot poffibly be doubted after the variety of evidence which has been adduced to that purpofe. Perrot, the old Sexton, who fucceeded Chatterton's great uncle, took Mr. Shiercliffe, a miniature painter, of Briftol, as early as the year 1749, through Redcliffe church; he fhewed him in the North porch a number of parchments, fome loofe and fome tied up, and intimated, " that there were things there, which would one day be better known; and that in proper hands, they might prove a treafure *." Many of the manufcripts

* Bryant's Obfervations, p. 513.

nufcripts in Mr. Barrett's hands bear all the marks of age, and are " figned by Rowley himfelf. The characters in each inftance appear to be fimilar; and the hand-writing the fame in all *."

IV. The fhort time which Chatterton had to produce all thefe poems, is an extraordinary circumftance. It has been already ftated, that he continued at Coulfton s fchool from the age of eight till that of fourteen and feven months : that he continued each day in fchool from feven or eight o'clock till twelve in the morning, and from one till four or five in the evening, and went to bed at eight. There is alfo reafon to believe, that he

did

Bryant's Obfervations p. 548. Mr. Barrett, and he only, has it in his power finally to determine the controverfy concerning Rowley's poems. Let him produce all the manufcripts which he obtained from Chatterton, and let them be put into the hands of fome perfons converfant in old writings, who may poffibly be able to decide concerning the probable date of the hand-writing. O.

did not difcover or begin to copy thefe
poems, or even to apply himfelf to antiquities, before the age of fifteen. In about
the fpace therefore of two years and a
half, he made himfelf mafter of the ancient language of this country; he produced more than two volumes of poetry,
which are publifhed, and about as many
compofitions, in profe and verfe, as would
nearly fill two volumes more. During
this time he muft have read a confiderable
variety of books. He was ftudying me-
dicine, heraldry, and other fciences; he
was practicing drawing; he copied a large
book of precedents; and Mr. Lambert's
bufinefs, though not extenfive, muft have
occupied at leaft fome part of his attention.   Which, therefore, is the eafier
fuppofition, fay the advocates for Rowley, that this almoft miracle of induftry
or ability was performed by a boy; or
that

that Chatterton really copied the poems from ancient documents * ?

V. Chat-

Of thefe old writings, which he is fuppofed to have tranfcribed from obfcure and almoft illegible manufcripts, (exclufive of his mifcellaneous and political writings,) the poetical alone fills 288 octavo pages in Mr. Tywrhitt's edition ; and perhaps there are others, with a quantity of profe writings which might fill another fuch volume.   See Milles's edition, p. 438.

Thefe muft have been tranfcribed by him, either in Mr. Lambert's office, or during the few hours he fpent at home with his mother in an evening.   Neither Mr. Lambert nor his mother or fifter, take upon them to fay, that they ever faw him this way employed.   When not engaged in the immediate bufinefs of his profeffion, he was employed by his mafter to copy forms and precedents, as well to improve him in the law as to keep him employed.   Of thefe law forms and precedents, Mr. Lambert has in his poffeffion a folio book containing 334 pages, clofely written by Chatterton ; alfo 36 pages in another.   In the noting book, 36 notarial acts ; and in the letter book, 38 letters copied.

Add to all this his *own* acknowledged compofitions, filling 240 pages in the printed copy, and perhaps as many more in manufcript not yet publifhed.

The greateft part of thefe compofitions, both under Rowley's name and his own, was written before he went to London, in April 1770, he being then aged 17 years and five months ; and of the former, Rowley's pieces, they were almoft all exhibited a twelve month earlier, before April 1769.

Now

V. Chatterton is faid further to have difcovered great marks of ignorance on the
manufcripts coming firft into his poffeffion.
He read the name *Roulie* inftead of Rowley,
till he was fet right by Mr. Barrett *.
In the acknowledged writings of Chatterton, there are alfo palpable miftakes, and
marks of ignorance in hiftory, geography,
&c.; whereas no fuch appear in the poems
of Rowley †.   But what is of ftill greater
confequence, Mr. Bryant has laboured to
prove, that in almoft innumerable inftances, Chatterton did not underftand the
language of Rowley, but that he has ac-
P   tually

Now the time taken up in preparing the parchment and
imitating the old writing, muft probably have been greater
than the time fpent in compofing them. If he was in poffeffion of the originals, furely he would not have beftowed
all this time and pains in tranfcribing from originals, which
he might have parted with to greater advantage; and if
he did tranfcribe them, why deftroy the greateft part of
them, and exhibit only fcraps and detached lines, for fuch
only appear now to exift ?   O.
  * Remarks on Warton, p. 9.
  † Bryant s Obfervations, p. 477.

tually mifinterpreted, and fometimes mif
tranfcribed him.   Thus in "the Englifh metamorphofis," ver. 14.

"Their myghte is *knopped* ynne the frofte of fere."

Chatterton having recourfe to Chaucer
and Skinner, has interpreted to *knop*, to *tie*,
or *faften* ; whereas it really means, and the
context requires that it fhould mean, to
nip.   Thus in the Second Battle of Haftings, 548, defcribing a facrifice :

"Roaftynge their *vyctualle* round about the flame ;"

which Mr. Tyrwhitt himfelf has allowed
ought to be *vyctimes*, and has accordingly
cancelled the other word.   Thus in Ella,
v. 678, we find :

"Theyre throngynge corfes fhall *onlyghte* the ftarres."

The word *onlyghte*, Chatterton has here
ftrangely applied as meaning to *darken* the
ftars, whereas Mr. Byrant, by recurring to
the Saxon, very reafonably fuppofes *on-
lych*

lych to have been the proper word, and the
line will then mean to *be like*, or to equal
the ftars in number. The word *cheri-
faunei*, which Chatterton has inferted in
the " Introductionne to Ella," never did
really exift, and Mr. Bryant fhews that
the original word was certainly *cherifaunce*:
and in the Second Eclogue, Chatterton
has explained the word *amenufed*, by *leff-
ened*, or *diminifhed*; whereas the fame able
critic fhews, that it never had any fuch
meaning, but that it really fignifies *ac-
curfed* or *abominable*. Thefe and other
fimilar miftakes (of which Mr. Bryant
fpecifies a great number) he afferts, could
never have happened, had Chatterton
been any more than the mere tranfcriber
of thefe extraordinary poems *

VI. With refpect to the objection, that
Rowley is not mentioned by other writers, it is anfwered, that there exifted fo

* See Mr. Bryant's Obfervations, paffim.

little communication among mankind at that time, that Leland, who is a very curious writer, never makes the fmalleft mention of Canynge, Lydgate, or Occleve. That William of Worceftre, does not mention Rowley, becaufe, unlefs hiftory demands it, writers do not commonly commemorate perfons before their death, and Rowley was apparently alive when William of Worceftre was at Briftol. In the regifter of the Diocefe of Wells, however, there are two perfons of the name of Thomas Rowley, mentioned as admitted into Holy Orders, one of whom might be the author of the poems *. In anfwer to the objection, why thefe manufcripts remained fo long unknown to the world, Mr. Bryant fays, " We may not be able to account any more for thefe manufcripts being fo long neglected, than for thofe of Hefychius, Phœdrus, and Velle-
                                    ius

* Mr. Bryant's Obf. p. 535, 543 544.

ius Paterculus having been in the fame
fituation * :" and with refpect to the fe-
creting of the originals by Chatterton, it
is deemed a fufficient reply, that he might
conceive very highly of their value, and
therefore did not wifh to part with them,
or he might be apprehenfive that they
would be taken from him; and at laft, in
his indignation againft the world, he probably deftroyed all of them that remained
at the time when he determined upon
putting an end to his exiftence.

VII. The conceffions of the adverfaries
ought not to pafs unnoticed on this occafion. Mr. Warton admits, " that fome
poems written by Rowley might have been
preferved in Canynge's cheft ; but if there
were any, they were fo enlarged and improved by Chatterton, as to become entirely new compofitions †;" and in a fub-

fequent

* Ibid, 499.
† Hiftory of Englifh Poetry.

fequent publication, fays, "I will not deny that Chatterton might difcover parchments of humble profe, containing local memoirs and authentic deeds, illuf- trating the hiftory of Briftol.   He might have difcovered biographical diaries, or other notices of the lives of Canynge, Ifcham, and Gorges" Thefe conceffions at leaft imply fomething of a doubt on the mind of the Laureat, concerning the ex- iftence of fome important manufcripts, and feem of fome confideration in the fcale of controverfy.

Internal Evidence in favour of the authen- ticity of Rowley's Poems.

I. The internal evidence (which we may call pofitive) on this fide of the quef- tion is not very extenfive, and the bulk of it confifts in negative arguments, or a refutation of the adverfaries' objections. The moft material proof is derived from

the

the ALLUSIONS TO FACTS and CUSTOMS, of which there is not much probability, that Chatterton could have a competent knowledge. Thus, if the " Dethe of Sir Charles Bawdin" be fuppofed, as Mr. Tyrwhitt himfelf thinks probable, to refer to the execution of Sir Baldwin of Fulford, the fact meets confirmation in all its circumftances, from a fragment publifhed by Hearne, and alfo from a parliamentary roll of the eighth of Edward IV; neither which there is the leaft probability that Chatterton ever faw*. Thus the names which occur in the Battle of Haftings, may almoft all be authenticated from the old hiftorians; but they are fcattered in fuch a variety of books, that they could not be extracted without infinite labour, and feveral of the books were in all probability not acceffible by Chatterton.

P 4   To

* Obfervations on Rowley's poems, p. 14.

To this head we may refer many particulars concerning Canynge, &c. as related by Chatterton, fuch as his paying
3000 marks to the king, *pro pace fua
habenda,* &c. which are confirmed in an
extraordinary manner by W. of Worceftre,
whofe book was not made public till 1778,
and which it was therefore impoffible
Chatterton could fee previous to the publication of his memoirs ; fuch is alfo the
time of Canynge's entering into Holy Orders, which is confirmed by the Epifco-
pal regifter of Worcefter ; and the anecdote of the fteeple of Redcliffe church
being burnt down by lightning in 1446.
Of a fimiliar kind is a circumftance in the
the orthography of the name *Fefcampe,*
(which is the right orthography,) while
Holingfhead, the only author acceffible to
Chatterton, has it *Flifchampe.* The name
of Robert Conful alfo, whom Rowley re-
prefents as having repaired the caftle of
Briftol,

Briftol, occurs in Leland, as the proprietor of that Caftle*.

II. With regard to the STYLE, COM-
POSITION, and SENTIMENT. If the
poems appear fuperior to the efforts of the]
firft fcholars at the revival of letters;
what are they, when confidered as the
productions of an uneducated charity boy,
not quite feventeen? Thofe alfo who think
that Chatterton could not reduce his genius
to the ftandard of the age of Rowley,
fhould, perhaps, rather wonder why he
could never raife his own avowed productions to an equal degree of excellence †.
The poems attributed to Rowley, if his,
are as much the work of his infantine
years, as his own mifcellaneous poems;
indeed,

---

* See Bryant's Obfervations, p. 314, 326, 343, &c.

† The moft effential difference that ftrikes me between
the poems of Rowley and Chatterton is, that the former
are always built upon fome confiftent interefting plot, and
are more *uniformly* excellent in the execution; the latter are
irregular fallies upon ill-felected or trifling fubjects.

indeed, many of the latter were compofed fome time after moft of Rowley's were exhibited to the world ; that they fhould be inferior in every excellence of poetry, is therefore a myftery not eafy to be accounted for. Againft the general propofition, that poetry like other arts is progreffive, and never arrived to perfection in an early age ; it has been judicioufly urged, that " Genius is peculiar neither to *age* nor country," but that we have an example of one man (Homer), who in the very infancy of all arts, without guide or precurfor, " gave to the world a work, which has been the admiration and model of all fucceeding poets †." And though it be admitted, that Rowley's poems are pervaded by an uniform ftrain of excellence and tafte, which does not appear in the other works of his age now extant, yet

when

---

* Matthias's Effay, p. 98.

when we compare any compofition with another of the fame or of any prior age, the difference fubfifting, will frequently be found not to depend upon *time*, but upon the fituation, genius and judgment of the refpective authors †.

III. As to METRE, it is faid, that in all languages the modes and meafures of verfe were originally invented and adopted from accidental circumftances, and agreeably to the tafte of different authors; and that very early in the Englifh poetry, a great variety of meafures are known to have prevailed, fuch is the octave ftanza, which is not many removes from the ufual ftanza of Rowley, the feven lined ftanza, or Rithm Royal, and that of ten lines ufed by Chaucer in one of his fmaller poems. The argument founded on the fmoothnefs of the verfe, is attempted to be overturned by Mr. Bryant,

* Matthias's Effay, p. 72.

Bryant, who has produced extracts from poems still older than the age of Rowley, which are deficient neither in harmony nor cadence *.

IV. The objection founded on the ancient LANGUAGE of Rowley, is answered by supposing that his language was probably provincial †. Several of the words objected to as of Chatterton's coining, have by more profound researches been traced in ancient writers. Many words in Rowley's poems cannot be found in those dictionaries and glossaries, to which Chatterton had access ‡, and Chatterton's mistakes in transcribing and explaining the old language of Rowley, have already been instanced.

V. Many of the pretended IMITATIONS of THE MODERN poets to be found

---

* Observations, p. 425, &c. 552.
† Ibid, p. 1, to 25.
‡ Matthias's Essay, p. 77.

found in Rowley, are objected to upon good grounds, as being ideas obvious to Rowley or any man; and as to the others, why may we not suppose them, " insertions of Chatterton, either to please his own ear, or to restore some parts which were lost, or in places where the words were difficult to be decypered *?" This argument acquires great weight, when the temper and genius of Chatterton is considered, and when it is recollected that all parties agree in the probability of many interpolations being made by him; and if this argument be admitted, it will in a great measure account for the modern phraselogy which so frequently occurs in these poems.

In rejoinder to these arguments, a few facts have been stated by those who sup-

port

* Matthias's Essay, p. 105.

port the title of Chatterton. 1ft. That no writings or cheft depofited in Redcliffe church are mentioned in Mr. Canynge's will, which has been carefully infpected, nor any books except two, called "Liggers cum integra legenda," which he leaves to be ufed occafionally in the choir by the two chaplains eftablifhed by him *, 2d. To account for Chatterton's extenfive acquaintance with old books out of the common line of reading, it is alledged that the old library at Briftol was, during his life time, of univerfal accefs, and Chatterton was actually introduced to it by the Rev. Mr. Catcott †. 3d. Chatterton's account of Canynge, &c. as far as it is countenanced by William of Worceftre, (that is, as far as refpects his taking orders and paying a fine to the king) may be found in the epitaph on Mafter Canynge, ftill remaining to be read by every perfon, both in

Latin

Tywrhitt's Vindication, p. 117.
† Warton's Inquiry, p. 111.

Latin and Englifh, in Redcliffe church, which indeed appears to be the authority, that William of Worceftre himfelf has followed. Chatterton's account alfo of Redcliffe fteeple, is to be found at the bottom of a print of that church, publifhed in 1746, by oné John Halfpenny; " in which was recounted the ruin of the fteeple in 1446, by a tempeft and fire *." 4th. As to the old vellum or parchment on which Chatterton tranfcribed his fragments, it is obferved, that " at the bottom of each fheet of old deeds, (of which there were many in the Briftol cheft) there is ufually a blank fpace of about four or five inches in breadth;" and this exactly agrees with the fhape and fize of the largeft fragment which he has exhibited, viz. Eight and a half inches long, and four and a-half broad +

* Tywrhitt's Vindication, p. 113, 212.
+ Curfory Obfervations, p. 29.

THUS

THUS I have exhibited as faithfully as I was able, an abſtract of the arguments on both ſides of this curious literary queſtion. To the examination I ſat down with a ſceptical mind; nor can I recollect being influenced during the progreſs of the inquiry in a ſingle inſtance, by the authority of names, by the force of ridicule, or the partialities of friendſhip. Some remarks, I believe, I may have added, which are not to be found in other books; in this, however, I am not conſcious of having favoured one party more than the other, but eſteemed it a part of my duty to ſtate the obſervations as they roſe in my mind from a conſideration of the facts. I ſhall not intrude upon my readers any verdict of my own concerning the iſſue of the controverſy; ſince my only intention was to enable them, from a view of the arguments, to form their own concluſions; leaving them ſtill open to

the

the impreſſion of any additional or more
ſatisfactory evidence that may hereafter
ariſe. I cannot, however, lay aſide my
pen without one general reflection. It is
impoſſible to peruſe the ſtate of this controverſy, without ſmiling at the folly and
vanity of poſthumous fame. The author
of theſe poems, whoever he was, certainly
never flattered himſelf with the expectation that they would ever excite half the
curioſity, or half the admiration which
they have excited in the literary world.
If they really be the productions of Rowley, one of the firſt, both in order and
in merit of our Engliſh poets, is defraud-
ed of more than half his reputation; if
they be the works of Chatterton, they
neither ſerved to raiſe him in the opinion
of his intimate acquaintance and friends,
nor to procure for him the comforts or
even the neceſſaries of life. He has de-
ſcended to his grave with a dubious cha-

Q   racter;

racter; and the only praife which can be accorded him by the warmeft of his admirers, is that of an elegant and ingenious impoftor.

For the fatisfaction of thofe readers, who may wifh to review the whole controverfy at large, and for the information of pofterity, I fubjoin the moft accurate lift I have been able to procure of all the publications which have appeared on both fides.

A Lift of the various Publications upon the Subject of ROWLEY'S POEMS, *for* and *againft* their *Authenticity*.

EDITIONS OF ROWLEY.

POEMS, fuppofed to have been written at Briftol by Thomas Rowley, and others, in the Fifteenth Century; the greateft Part now firft publifhed from the moft authentic Copies, with an engraved Specimen of one of the MS.   To which are added, a Preface, an Introductory Account of the feveral Pieces, and a Gloffary.   Ed. 8vo. 1777.

N. B. This Edition has been reprinted.

Ditto: with a Commentary, in which the Antiquity of them is confidered and defended, by Jeremiah Milles, D. D. Dean of Exeter. Ed. 4to. 1782.

THE

THE EIGHTH Section of Mr. Warton's Second Volume of the History of English Poetry, with the Notes to it.

REMARKS on the Eighth Section of Mr. Warton's Second Volume of the history of English Poetry.
Payne, Mews-Gate.

Two Letters by the Hon. Mr. Horace Walpole; printed at Strawberry-hill.—Reprinted, (by his permission) in the Gentleman's Magazines for April, May, June, July, 1782.

APPENDIX, containing some Observations upon the Language of the Poems attributed to Rowley, tending to prove, that they were written not by any ancient Author, but entirely by Thomas Chatterton. *Payne, Mews-Gate.*

N. B. This Appendix is *now* generally annexed to the 8vo. Edition of Rowley's Poems.

OBSERVATIONS on the Poems attributed to Rowley, tending to prove, that they were really written by Him and other Ancient Authors. To which are added, Remarks on the Appendix of the Editor (of the 8vo. Ed). of Rowley's Poems. *Bathurst, Fleet-Street.*

OBSERVATIONS upon the Poems of Thomas Rowley; in which the Authenticity of those Poems is ascertained. By Jacob Bryant, Esq. *Payne, Mews-Gate, &c.*

CURSORY Observations on the Poems attributed to Thomas Rowley, a Priest in the fifteenth Century: with some Remarks on the Commentaries on these Poems, by the Reverend Dr. Jeremiah Milles, Dean of Exeter, and Jacob Bryant, Esq. *Nichols and Walter, Charing-cross.*

AN ENQUIRY into the Authenticity of the Poems attributed to Thomas Rowley, in which the Arguments of the

Q 2   Dean

Dean of Exeter and Mr. Bryant are examined.   By Thomas Warton, Fellow of Trinity College, Oxford, and F. S. A.   *Dodsley, Pall-Mall.*

Strictures upon a Pamphlet entitled, " Cursory Observations on the Poems attributed to Rowley, a Priest in the Fifteenth Century." With a Postscript on Mr. Thomas Warton's Enquiry into the same Subject. By. E. B. Greene, Esq.   *Stockdale, Piccadilly.*

A Vindication of the Appendix to the Poems called Rowley's : In Reply to the Answers of the Dean of Exeter, Jacob Bryant Esq. and a third anonymous Writer; with some further observations upon those Poems, and an Examination of the Evidence which has been produced in Support of their Authenticity.   By Thomas Tyrwhitt.
                                  Payne, Mew's-Gate.

An Essay on the Evidence, External and Internal, relating to the Poems attributed to Thomas Rowley and others, in the Fifteenth Century, containing a general View of the whole Controversy.   By Thomas James Mathias.
                                  Becket, Pall Mall.

To which may be added various shorter Compositions on the Subject (too numerous to specify) inserted in the different monthly Magazines.

APPENDIX.

APPENDIX.

The following Poem was copied from a manuscript of CHATTERTON, *and the Editor believes has never before been presented to the Public.*

The ART of PUFFING,

By a BOOKSELLER's JOURNEYMAN.

VERS'D by experience in the subtle art,
The myst'ries of a title I impart :
Teach the young author how to please the town;
And make the heavy drug of rhime go down.
Since Curl, immortal, never dying name,
A double pica in the book of fame,
By various arts did various dunces prop,
And tickled every fancy to his shop :
Who can like Pottinger ensure a book ?
Who judges with the solid taste of Cooke ?
Villains exalted in the midway sky,
Shall live again, to drain your purses dry :
Nor yet unrivall'd they; see Baldwin comes,
Rich in inventions, patents, cuts and hums :
The honorable Boswell writes, 'tis true,
What else can Paoli's supporter do ?

The

The trading wits endeavour to attain,
Like bookfellers, the world's firft idol—gain:
For this they puff the heavy Goldfmith's line,
And hail his fentiment tho' trite, divine ;
For this, the patriotic bard complains,
And Bingley binds poor liberty in chains :
For this was every reader's faith deceiv'd,
And Edmund fwore what nobody believ'd :
For this the wits in clofe difguifes fight ;
For this the varying politicians write ;
For this each month new magazines are fold,
With dullnefs fill'd and tranfcripts of the old.
The Town and Country ftruck a lucky hit,
Was novel, fentimental, full of wit :
Apeing her walk, the fame fuccefs to find,
The Court and City hobbles far behind :
Sons of Apollo learn, merit's no more
Than a good frontifpiece to grace her door ;
The author who invents a title well,
Will always find his cover'd dullnefs fell ;
Flexney and every bookfeller will buy, —
Bound in neat calf, the work will never die.

V A M P.

July 22, 1770.

LETTERS

LETTERS

OF

THOMAS CHATTERTON.

LETTER I.

London, April 26, 1770.

Dear Mother,

HERE I am, safe, and in high spirits
—To give you a journal of my tour
would not be unnecessary. After riding
in the basket to Brislington, I mounted
the top of the coach, and rid easy; and
agreeably entertained with the conversa-
tion of a quaker *in dress*, but little so in
personals and behaviour. This laughing
friend, who is a carver, lamented his
having sent his tools to Worcester, as
otherwise he would have accompanied me

Q 4

to

to London. I left him at Bath; when, finding it rained pretty faſt, I entered an inſide paſſenger to Speenhamland, the half-way ſtage, paying ſeven ſhillings. 'Twas lucky I did ſo, for it ſnowed all night, and on Marlborough Downs the ſnow was near a foot high.

At ſeven in the morning I breakfaſted at Speenhamland, and then mounted the coach-box for the remainder of the day, which was a remarkable fine one. — Honeſt gee-ho complimented me with aſſuring me, that I ſat bolder and tighter than any perſon who ever rid with him. —Dined at Stroud moſt luxuriantly, with a young gentleman who had ſlept all the preceding night in the machine; and an old mercantile genius, whoſe ſchool-boy ſon had a great deal of wit, as the father thought, in remarking that Windſor was as old as *our Saviour's time.*

Got

Got into London about five o'clock in the evening—called upon Mr. Edmunds, Mr. Fell, Mr. Hamilton, and Mr. Dodsley. Great encouragement from them; all approved of my defign;—fhall foon be fettled.——Call upon Mr. Lambert; fhew him this, or tell him, if I deferve a recommendation, he would oblige me to give me one—if I do not, it will be beneath him to take notice of me. Seen all aunts, coufins—all well—and I am welcome. Mr. T. Wenfley is alive, and coming home.——Sifter, grandmother, &c. &c. &c. remember.—I remain,

Your dutiful fon,

T. Chatterton.

LETTER

L E T T E R II.

Shoreditch, London, May 6, 1770.

Dear Mother,

I am furprifed that no letter has been fent in anfwer to my laft. I am fettled, and in fuch a fettlement as I would defire. I get four guineas a month by one Magazine: fhall engage to write a Hiftory of England, and other pieces, which will more than double that fum. Occafional effays for the daily papers would more than fupport me. What a glorious profpect! Mr. Wilkes knew me by my writings fince I firft correfponded with the bookfellers here. I fhall vifit him next week, and by his intereft will infure Mrs. Ballance the Trinity-Houfe. He affirmed that what Mr. Fell had of mine could not be the writings of a youth; and expreffed a defire to know the author. By the means of another

bookfeller

bookseller I shall be introduced to Townf-
hend and Sawbridge.   I am quite familiar
at the Chapter Coffee-house, and know
all the geniuses there.   A character is
now unneceffary; an author carries his
character in his pen.   My fister will improve herself in drawing.   My grandmother is, I hope, well.   Briftol's mercenary walls were never deftined to hold
me—there, I was out of my element;
now, I am in it—London! Good God!
how fuperior is London to that defpicable place Briftol!—Here is none of your
little meannesses, none of your mercenary
fecurities, which difgrace that miferable
hamlet.—Drefs, which is in Briftol an
eternal fund of fcandal, is here only introduced as a fubject of praife; if a man
dreffes well, he has tafte; if carelefs, he
has his own reafons for fo doing, and is
prudent.   Need I remind you of the
contraft?   The poverty of authors is a
                                    common

common obfervation, but not always a true one. No author can be poor who underftands the arts of bookfellers— Without this neceffary knowledge, the greateft genius may ftarve; and, with it, the greateft dunce live in fplendor. This knowledge I have pretty well dipped into. — The Levant man of war, in which T. Wenfley went out, is at Portf-mouth; but no news from him yet.— I lodge in one of Mr. Walmfley's beft rooms. Let Mr. Cary copy the letters on the other fide, and give them to the perfons for whom they are defigned, if nqt too much labour for him.

I remain, yours, &c.

T. Chatterton.

P. S. I have fome trifling prefents for my mother, fifter Thorne, &c.

Sunday morning,

For

For Mr. T C a r y.

I have fent you a tafk. I hope no unpleafing one. Tell all your acquaintance for the future to read the Freeholder's Magazine. When you have any thing for publication, fend it to me, and it fhall moft certainly appear in fome periodical compilation. Your laft piece was, by the ignorance of a corrector, jumbled under the confiderations in the acknowledgements. But I refcued it, and infifted on its appearance.

Your friend,

T. C.

Direct for me, to be left at the Chapter Coffee-houfe, Pater-nofter-row.

Mr. H e n r y K a t o r.

If you have not forgot Lady Betty, any Complaint, Rebus, or Enigma, on the dear charmer, directed for me, to be left at

the

the Chapter Coffee-houſe, Pater-noſter-row—ſhall find a place in ſome Magazine, or other; as I am engaged in many.

Your friend,

T. Chatterton.

Mr. WILLIAM SMITH.

When you have any poetry for publication, ſend it to me, to be left at the Chapter Coffee-houſe, Pater-noſter-row, and it ſhall moſt certainly appear.

Your friend,

T. C.

Mrs. BAKER.

The ſooner I ſee you the better—ſend me as ſoon as poſſible Rymſdyk's addreſs.

(Mr. Cary will leave this at Mr. Flower's, Small-ſtreet.)

Mr. MASON.

Give me a ſhort proſe deſcription of the ſituation of Naſh—and the poetic addition
ſhall

shall appear in some Magazine. Send me
also whatever you would have published,
and direct for me, to be left at the Chapter Coffee-house, Pater-noster-row.

Your friend,

T. Chatterton.

Mr. MAT. MEASE.

Begging Mr. Meafe's pardon for making
public ufe of his name lately—I hope he
will remember me, and tell all his acquaintance to read the Freeholder's Magazine for the future.

T. Chatterton.

TELL——

Mr. Thaire   Mr. Rudhall Mr. Ward
Mr. Gafter   Mr. Thomas   Mr. Kalo
Mr. A. Broughton Mr. Carty   Mr. Smith
Mr. J. Broughton Mr. Hanmor &c. &c.
Mr. Williams   Mr. Vaughan

to read the Freeholder's Magazine.

LETTER

LETTER III.

King's Bench, for the prefent, May 14, 1770.

Dear Madam,

Don't be furprized at the name of the place. I am not here as a prifoner. Matters go on fwimmingly : Mr. Fell having offended certain perfons, they have fet his creditors upon him, and he is fafe in the King's Bench. I have been bettered by this accident : His fucceffors in the Freeholder's Magazine, knowing nothing of the matter, will be glad to engage me, on my own terms. Mr. Edmunds has been tried before the Houfe of Lords, fentenced to pay a fine, and thrown into Newgate. His misfortunes will be to me of no little fervice. Laft week, being in the pit of Drury Lane, Theatre, I contracted an immediate acquaintance (which you know is no hard tafk to me) with a young gentle-

man

man in Cheapfide; partner in a mufic
fhop, the greateft in the city. Hearing I
could write, he defired me to write a few
fongs for him : this I did the fame night,
and conveyed them to him the next morning. Thefe he fhewed to a Doctor in
Mufic, and I am invited to treat with this
Doctor, on the footing of a compofer, for
Ranelagh and the Gardens. *Bravo, hey
boys, up we go!* — Befides the advantage
of vifiting thefe expenfive and polite places
gratis ; my vanity will be fed with the
fight of my name in copper-plate, and my
fifter will receive a bundle of printed fongs,
the words by her brother. Thefe are not
all my acquifitions : a gentleman who
knows me at the Chapter, as an author,
would have introduced me as a companion
to the young Duke of Northumberland,
in his intended general tour. But, alas!
I fpeak no tongue but my own ! — But
to return once more to a place I am

R   fickened

sickened to write of, Briftol. Though, as
an apprentice, none had greater liberties,
yet the thoughts of fervitude killed me:
now I have that for my labour, I always
reckoned the firft of my pleafures, and
have ftill, my liberty. As to the clearance,
I am ever ready to give it; but really I
underftand fo little of the law, that I believe Mr. Lambert muft draw it. Mrs.
L. brought what you mention. Mrs.
Hughes is as well as age will permit her
to be, and my coufin does very well.

I will get fome patterns worth your
acceptance; and wifh you and my fifter
would improve yourfelves in drawing, as
it is here a valuable and never-failing acquifition.———My box fhall be attended
to; I hope my books are in it—if not,
fend them; and particularly Catcott's
Hutchinfonian jargon on the Deluge, and
the M.S. Gloffary, compofed of one
fmall book, annexed to a larger.———My
fifter

ſiſter will remember me to Miſs Sandford.
I have not quite forgot her; though there
are ſo many pretty milleners, &c. that
I have almoſt forgot myſelf.——Carty
will think on me: upon inquiry, I find
his trade dwindled into nothing here.
A man may very nobly ſtarve by it; but
he muſt have luck indeed, who can live
by it.——Miſs Rumſey, if ſhe comes to
London, would do well, as an old acquaintance, to ſend me her addreſs.——
London is not Briſtol—We may patrole
the town for a day, without raiſing one
whiſper, or nod of ſcandal.—If ſhe re-
fuſes, the curſe of all antiquated virgins
light on her: may ſhe be refuſed, when
ſhe ſhall requeſt! Miſs Rumſey will tell
Miſs Baker, and Miſs Baker will tell Miſs
Porter, that Miſs Porter's favoured humble ſervant, though but a *young* man, is a
very old lover; and in the eight-and-
fiftieth year of his age: but that, as Lap-

R 2   pet

pet fays, is the flower of a man's days;
and when a lady can't get a young hufband, fhe muft put up with an old bed-
fellow. I left Mifs Singer, I am forry
to fay it, in a very bad way; that is, in a
way to be married.——But mum—Afk
Mifs Suky Webb the reft; if fhe knows,
fhe'll tell ye.—I beg her pardon for re-
vealing the fecret; but when the knot is
faftened, fhe fhall know how I came by
it.—Mifs Thatcher may depend upon it,
that, if I am not in love with her, I am
in love with nobody elfe: I hope fhe is
well; and if that whining, fighing, dying pulpit-fop, Lewis, has not finifhed
his languifhing lectures, I hope fhe will
fee her amorofo next Sunday.—If Mifs
Love has no objection to having a crambo
fong on her name publifhed, it fhall be
done. — Begging pardon of Mifs Cotton
for whatever has happened to offend her,
I can affure her it has happened without

my

my confent. I did not give her this af-
furance when in Briftol, left it fhould
feem like an attempt to avoid the anger
of her *furious* brother. Inquire, when
you can, how Mifs Broughton received
her billet. Let my fifter fend me a journal of all the tranfactions of the females
within the circle of your acquaintance.
Let Mifs Watkins know, that the letter
fhe made herfelf ridiculous by, was never
intended for her; but another young lady
in the neighbourhood, of the fame name.
I promifed, before my departure, to write
to fome hundreds, I believe; but, what
with writing for publications, and going
to places of public diverfion, which is
as abfolutely neceffary to me as food, I
find but little time to write to you. As
to Mr. Barrett, Mr. Catcott, Mr. Bur-
gum, &c. &c. they rate literary lumber
fo low, that I believe an author, in their
eftimation, muft be poor indeed! But

R 3   here

here matters are otherwife; had Rowley been a Londoner, inftead of a Briftowyan, I could have lived by copying his works. ———In my humble opinion, I am under very few obligations to any perfons in Briftol: one, indeed, has obliged me; but, as moft do, in a manner which makes his obligation no obligation.——My youthful acquaintances will not take it in dudgeon, that I do not write oftener to them, than I believe I fhall: but, as I had the happy art of pleafing in converfation, my company was often liked, where I did not like: and to continue a correfpondence under fuch circumftances, would be ridiculous. Let my fifter improve in copying mufic, drawing, and every thing which requires genius: in Briftol's mercantile ftyle thofe things may be ufelefs, if not a detriment to her; but here they are highly profitable.——Inform Mr. Rhife that nothing fhall be wanting, on my

part,

part, in the bufinefs he was fo kind as to employ me in; fhould be glad of a line from him, to know whether he would engage in the marine department; or fpend the reft of his days, fafe, on dry ground.—Intended waiting on the Duke of Bedford relative to the Trinity-Houfe; but his Grace is dangeroufly ill. My grandmother, I hope, enjoys the ftate of health I left her in. I am Mifs Webb's humble fervant. Thorne fhall not be forgot, when I remit the fmall trifles to you. Notwithftanding Mrs. B's not being able to inform me of Mr. Garfed's addrefs, through the clofenefs of the pious Mr. Ewer, I luckily ftumbled upon it this morning.

I remain, &c. &c. &c. &c.

Monday Evening.   Thomas Chatterton.

(Direct for me, at Mr. Walmfley's, at Shoreditch—only.)

R 4   LETTER

L E T T E R IV.

Tom's Coffee-houſe, London, May 30, 1770.

Dear Siſter,

There is ſuch a noiſe of buſineſs and politicks in the room, that my inaccuracy in writing here, is highly excuſable. My preſent profeſſion obliges me to frequent places of the beſt reſort. To begin with, what every female converſation begins with, dreſs: I employ my money now in fitting myſelf faſhionably, and getting into good company; this laſt article always brings me in intereſt. But I have engaged to live with a gentleman, the brother of a Lord (a Scotch one indeed), who is going to advance pretty deeply into the bookſelling branches: I ſhall have lodging and boarding, genteel and elegant, gratis: this article, in the quarter of the town he lives, with worſe accommodations, would be 50l. per annum.

I ſhall

I fhall have, likewife, no inconfiderable premium; and affure yourfelf every month fhall end to your advantage : I will fend you two filks this fummer ; and expect, in anfwer to this, what colours you prefer. My mother fhall not be forgotten. My employment will be writing a voluminous Hiftory of London, to appear in numbers the beginning of the next winter. As this will not, like writing political effays, oblige me to go to the coffeehoufe, I fhall be able to ferve you the more by it : but it will neceffitate me to go to Oxford, Cambridge, Lincoln, Coventry, and every collegiate church near ; not at all difagreeable journeys, and not to me expenfive. The Manufcript Gloffary, I mentioned in my laft, muft not be omitted. If money flowed as faft upon me as honours, I would give you a portion of 5000 l. You have, doubtlefs, heard of the Lord Mayor's remonftrating

and

and addreffing the King : but it will be a piece of news, to inform you that I have been with the Lord Mayor on the occafion. Having addreffed an effay to his Lordfhip, it was very well received; perhaps better than it deferved; and I waited on his Lordfhip, to have his approbation, to addrefs a fecond letter to him, on the fubject of the remonftrance, and its reception. His Lordfhip received me as politely as a citizen could; and warmly invited me to call on him again. The reft is a fecret———But the devil of the matter is, there's no money to be got of this fide the queftion. Intereft is of the other fide. But he is a poor author, who cannot write on both fides. I believe I may be introduced (and, if I am not, I'll introduce myfelf) to a ruling power in the Court party. I might have a recommendation to Sir George Colebrook, an Eaft-India Director, as quali-
fied

APPENDIX. 251

fied for an office no ways defpicable; but
I fhall not take a ftep to the fea, whilft I
can continue on land. I went yefterday
to Woolwich, to fee Mr. Wenfley; he is
paid to-day. The artillery is no unpleafing fight, if we bar reflection, and do
not confider how much mifchief it may
do. Greenwich Hofpital and St. Paul's
Cathedral are the only ftructures which
could reconcile me to any thing out of
the Gothic. Mr. Carty will hear from
me foon: multiplicity of literary bufinefs muft be my excufe. — I condole with
him, and my dear Mifs Sandford, in the
misfortune of Mrs. Carty: my phyfical
advice is, to leech her temples plenti-
fully: keep her very low in diet; as
much in the dark as poffible. Nor is
this laft prefcription the whim of an old
woman: whatever hurts the eyes, affects
the brain: and the particles of light,
                                    when

when the fun is in the fummer figns, are
highly prejudicial to the eyes; and it is
from this fympathetic effect, that the
head-ach is general in fummer. But,
above all, talk to her but little, and never contradict her in any thing. This
may be of fervice. I hope it will. Did
a paragraph appear in your paper of Saturday laft, mentioning the inhabitants of
London's having opened another view of
St. Paul's; and advifing the corporation,
or veftry of Redclift, to procure a more
compleat view of Redclift church? My
compliments to Mifs Thatcher : if I am
in love, I am; though the devil take me,
if I can tell with whom it is. I believe
I may addrefs her in the words of Scripture, which no doubt fhe reveres; " If
you had not ploughed with my heifer"
(or bullock rather), " you had not found
out my riddle." Humbly thanking Mifs
                                        Rumfey

Rumfey for her complimentary expreffion,
I cannot think it fatisfactory. Does fhe,
or does fhe not, intend coming to London? Mrs. O'Coffin has not yet got a
place; but there is not the leaft doubt
but fhe will in a little time.

Effay-writing has this advantage, you
are fure of conftant pay; and when you
have once wrote a piece which makes the
author enquired after, you may bring the
bookfellers to your own terms. Effays
on the patriotic fide fetch no more than
what the copy is fold for. As the patriots
themfelves are fearching for a place, they
have no gratuities to fpare. So fays one
of the beggars, in a temporary alteration
of mine, in the Jovial Crew:

> A patriot was my occupation,
>   It got me a name but no pelf:
> Till, ftarv'd for the good of the nation,
>   I begg'd for the good of myfelf.
>   Fal, lal, &c.

I toid

I told them, if 'twas not for me,
  Their freedoms would all go to pot;
I promis'd to set them all free,
  But never a farthing I got.
                              Fal, lal, &c.

—On the other hand, unpopular essays
will not even be accepted; and you must
pay to have them printed: but then you
seldom lose by it. Courtiers are so sen-
sible of their deficiency in merit, that
they generally reward all who know how
to daub them with an appearance of it.
To return to private affairs —— Friend
Slude may depend upon my endeavouring
to find the publications you mention.
They publish the Gospel Magazine here.
For a whim I write in it. I believe there
are not any sent to Bristol; they are hardly worth the carriage—methodistical, and
unmeaning. With the usual ceremonies
to my mother, and grandmother; and sin-
cerely, without ceremony, wishing them
                                    both

both happy; when it is in my power to make them so, they shall be so; and with my kind remembrance to Miss Webb, and Miss Thorne; I remain, as I ever was,

Yours, &c. to the end of the chapter,

Thomas Chatterton.

P. s. I am this minute pierced through the heart by the black eye of a young lady, driving along in a Hackney-coach. —— I am quite in love : if my love lasts till that time, you shall hear of it in my next.

LETTER V.

June 19, 1770.

Dear Sister,

I have an horrid cold —— The relation of the manner of my catching it may give you more pleasure than the circumstance itself. As I wrote very late Sunday night

night (or rather very early Monday morning), I thought to have gone to bed
pretty foon laft night: when, being half
undreffed, I heard a very doleful voice,
finging Mifs Hill's favorite bedlamite
fong. The hum-drum of the voice fo
ftruck me, that though I was obliged to
liften a long while before I could hear
the words, I found the fimilitude in the
found. After hearing her with pleafure
drawl for above half an hour, fhe jumped
into a brifker tune, and hobbled out the
ever-famous fong, in which poor Jack
Fowler was to have been fatirized. ——
" I put my hand into a bufh: I prick'd
" my finger to the bone: I faw a fhip
" failing along: I thought the fweeteft
" flowers to find:" and other pretty
flowery expreffions, were twanged with
no inharmonious bray.——I now ran to
the window, and threw up the fafh; re-
folved to be fatisfied, whether or no it

was

was the identical Mifs Hill, *in propria
perſōna.*——But, alas! it was a perfon
whofe twang is very well known, when
ſhe is awake, but who had drank fo much
royal bob (the gingerbread-baker for that,
you know), that ſhe was now finging herfelf afleep. This fomnifying liquor had
made her voice fo like the fweet echo of
Mifs Hill's, that if I had not confidered
that ſhe could not fee her way up to
London, I ſhould abfolutely have ıma-
gined it hers —— There was a fellow and
a girl in one corner, more bufy in at-
tending to their own affairs, than the
melody.

*This part of the letter, for ſome lines,
is not legible.*

. . . . . . the morning) from Marybone
gardens; I faw the fellow in the cage at
the watch-houfe, in the pariſh of St.
Giles; and the nymph is an inhabitant of
one of Cupid's inns of Court.——There
was one fimilitude it would be injuftice

S

to let flip. A drunken fifhman, who fells
foufe mackarel, and other delicious dain-
ties, to the eternal detriment of all two-
penny ordinaries; as his beft commodity,
his falmon, goes off at three halfpence
the piece: this itinerant merchant, this
moveable fifh-ftall, having likewife had
his dofe of bob-royal, ftood ftill for a
while; and then joined chorus, in a tone
which would have laid half a dozen law-
yers, pleading for their fees, faft afleep:
this naturally reminded me of Mr. Hay-
thorne's fong of

" Says Plato, who oy oy oy fhould man be vain ?"

However, my entertainment, though
fweet enough in itfelf has a difh of four
fauce ferved up in it; for I have a moft
horrible wheezing in the throat : but I
don't repent that I have this cold; for
there are fo many noftrums here, that 'tis
worth a man's while to get a diftemper,
he can be cured fo cheap.

June 29th, 1770.

My

My cold is over and gone. If the above did not recall to your mind fome fcenes of laughter, you have loft your ideas of rifibility.

L E T T E R VI.*

Dear Mother,

I fend you in the box — fix cups and faucers with two bafons, for my fifter — If a china tea pot and cream pot, is in your opinion, neceffary, I will fend them, but I am informed they are unfafhionable, and that the red china, which you are provided with, is more in ufe——a cargo of patterns, for yourfelf, with a fnuff box, right French and very curious in my opinion.

S 2   Two

* Chatterton had probably changed his lodging a little before he wrote this letter. It is a remarkable paffage where he fays, he wifhes fhe had fent him up his red pocket book, "as 'tis very material." "More graver," in the 13th line, confirms Mr. Bryant's opinion, p. 481, "that he was not well grounded in the firft principles of Grammar."

Two fans—the silver one, is more graver than the other, which would suit my sister best——But that I leave to you both.

Some British herb snuff, in the box; be careful how you open it—(This I omit lest it injure the other matters)

Some British herb tobacco for my grandmother, some trifles for Thorne. Be assured whenever I have the power, my will won't be wanting to testify, that I remember you——

Yours,

July 8, 1770.   T. Chatterton.

N. B.—I shall forestall your intended journey, and pop down upon you at Christmas——

I could have wished, you had sent my red pocket book, as 'tis very material

I bought two very curious twisted pipes for my grandmother; but both breaking; I was afraid to buy others lest they should

break

break in the box; and being loose, injure the china. Have you heard any
thing further of the clearance——

Direct for me at Mrs. Angels', Sack-maker, Brooke
Street, Holborn.

" Mrs. Chatterton."

LETTER VII.

Dear Sifter,

I have sent you some china and a fan.
You have your choice of two. I am furprifed that you chose purple and gold. I
went into the fhop to buy it: but it is
the most disagreeable colour I ever saw—
dead, lifeless, and inelegant. Purple and
pink, or lemon and pink, are more genteel and lively. Your answer in this af-
fair will oblige me. Be assured, that I
shall ever make your wants, my wants;
and stretch to the utmost to serve you.
Remember me to Mifs Sandford, Mifs
Rumfey, Mifs Singer, &c. &c. &c.

As

As to the fongs, I have waited this week for them, and have not had time to copy one perfectly: when the feafon's over, you will have 'em all in print. I had pieces laft month in the following Magazines:

> Gofpel Magazine,
> Town and Country, viz.
>> Maria Friendlefs.
>> Falfe Step.
>> Hunter of Oddities,
> To Mifs Bufh, &c.

> Court and City. London. Political Regifter, &c. &c.

The Chriftian Magazine, as they are not to be had perfect, are not worth buying——I remain,

> Yours,
>> T. Chatterton.

July 11, 1770.

L E T-

LETTER VIII.

I am now about an Oratorio, which,
when finished, will purchafe you a gown.
You may be certain of feeing me before
the 1ft of January, 1771.—The clearance is immaterial.—My mother may expect more patterns.—Almoft all the next
Town and Country Magazine is mine.
I have an univerfal acquaintance:—my
company is courted every where; and,
could I humble myfelf to go into a
compter, could have had twenty places
before now:—but I muft be among the
great; ftate matters fuit me better than
commercial. The ladies are not out of
my acquaintance. I have a deal of bufinefs now, and muft therefore bid you
adieu. You will have a longer letter from
me foon——and more to the purpofe.

Yours,
T. C.

20th July, 1770.

F I N I S.

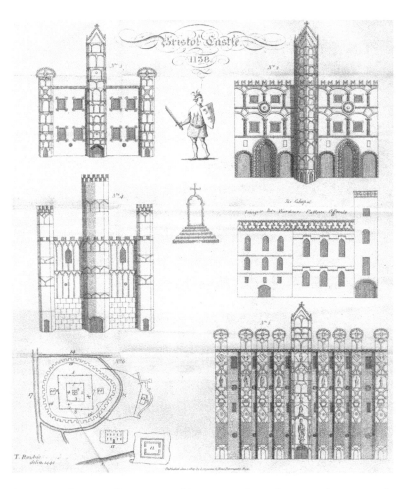

The material originally positioned here is too large for reproduction in this reissue. A PDF can be downloaded from the web address given on page iv of this book, by clicking on 'Resources Available'.

For EU product safety concerns, contact us at Calle de José Abascal, 56–1°,
28003 Madrid, Spain or eugpsr@cambridge.org.

www.ingramcontent.com/pod-product-compliance
Ingram Content Group UK Ltd.
Pitfield, Milton Keynes, MK11 3LW, UK
UKHW010344140625
459647UK00010B/823